Leonard Bernstein

Titles in the series Critical Lives present the work of leading cultural figures of the modern period. Each book explores the life of the artist, writer, philosopher or architect in question and relates it to their major works.

In the same series

Leonard Bernstein

Paul R. Laird

REAKTION BOOKS

This book is dedicated to Charles Atkinson, Herbert S. Livingston and James W. Pruett, who started me down the scholarly path

Published by Reaktion Books Ltd
Unit 32, Waterside
44–48 Wharf Road
London N1 7UX, UK

www.reaktionbooks.co.uk

First published 2018
Copyright © Paul R. Laird 2018

Printed and bound in Great Britain by Bell & Bain, Glasgow

A catalogue record for this book is available from the British Library

ISBN 978 1 78023 910 1

Contents

Introduction

The multifaceted career of Leonard Bernstein can hardly be reduced
to six moments, but his formation as a musician of profound, varied
talents can be illuminated by brief consideration of five moments
from his early career, and one event late in his life that is most
informative about the world-famous figure that he became. The
nearly five decades between these occasions included one of the
most extraordinary musical careers of the last few centuries, which
was made possible by the talents and self-confidence manifested
early in his life.

On 17 February 1943 the 24-year-old Bernstein, virtually
unknown at this point, replaced Aaron Copland as performer
of his Piano Sonata at a Town Hall Music Forum in New York
dedicated to the composer, where two of his orchestral suites were
also performed. Copland was unable to leave California, where
he was working on a film score, and, not long before the forum,
he deputized his young friend to play the sonata. Bernstein, an
outstanding pianist with a special feeling for Copland's music,
quickly worked up a fine performance that impressed New
York's musical elite. Then, according to reports, he made strong
contributions in the panel discussion that followed.

After being named assistant conductor of the New York
Philharmonic by the new music director Artur Rodzinski in late
August 1943, on 14 November Bernstein walked onto the stage
of Carnegie Hall to lead a nationally broadcast concert with the

orchestra. The audience was expecting the distinguished German conductor Bruno Walter, but instead they witnessed the spectacular debut of a young American conductor entirely trained in the United States. The event was front-page news in the New York papers the next day, and a little more than two months after taking a position that did not often grant a musician prominence, Bernstein was famous.

Within three weeks in the winter of 1944, Bernstein conducted the premiere of his 'Jeremiah' Symphony with the Pittsburgh Symphony Orchestra – an ensemble led by Fritz Reiner, who had been Bernstein's conducting professor at the Curtis Institute of Music – and then with the Boston Symphony Orchestra, led by Bernstein's mentor Serge Koussevitzky. The work triumphed in both cities.

Only a few months later, Bernstein emerged as composer of a consequential ballet score, *Fancy Free*, with choreography by Jerome Robbins. It premiered at the Metropolitan Opera House on 18 April 1944. Involving an evening in a bar for three American sailors on leave in wartime New York, the ballet was superbly appropriate for the moment and became a smash hit. Impresario Sol Hurok extended the season in the enormous venue by two weeks to accommodate the audiences, and then *Fancy Free* went on tour.

The scenario of *Fancy Free* became a Broadway musical, *On the Town*, which premiered on 28 December 1944. Robbins again was the choreographer while Bernstein worked on the score with two friends, lyricists Betty Comden and Adolph Green, who also wrote the book. Broadway director George Abbott was the experienced hand who inspired the project's necessary investment, which was a major hit and ran for 462 performances.

Five opportunities, all within less than two years, where Bernstein demonstrated his huge talents in the five areas where he became famous: pianist, commentator, conductor, composer in classical genres such as the symphony and ballet scores, and composer of a Broadway musical. Certainly musicians with multiple talents had exploded onto musical scenes before Bernstein, but never so publicly or in such diverse areas in the United States, and by the end of the 1940s his conducting career was an international phenomenon in Europe and in the new nation of Israel. With huge success to follow as a music educator on American television, Broadway musicals like *West Side Story*, his famous tenure as music director of the New York Philharmonic and his work with the Vienna Philharmonic, Bernstein fashioned one of the most distinctive musical careers in the Western world in the decades after the Second World War.

A fascinating measurement of Bernstein's fame and significance occurred following the fall of the Berlin Wall in 1989. Along with his business organization, the conductor assembled a televised and recorded rendition of Beethoven's Symphony no. 9 in the Schauspielhaus in East Berlin on Christmas Day. He brought together a quartet of vocal soloists, the Bavarian Radio Symphony Orchestra and Chorus and, in an extraordinarily symbolic gesture, members of orchestras from Dresden, Leningrad, London, New York and Paris, representing East Germany and the countries that had occupied defeated Berlin and the remainder of Germany a bit more than four decades before. Bernstein changed the symphony's text to celebrate the occasion, making Schiller's famed 'Ode to Joy' exclaim 'O Freiheit' (Oh freedom) rather than 'O Freude' (Oh joy), a cheeky interpolation but completely consistent with Bernstein's conception of the moment. That an American Jewish conductor produced this event seems almost unbelievable to this day.

The picture of Leonard Bernstein that emerges in the following pages covers the public Bernstein, steward and benefactor of the titanic gifts that made his career possible. In a biography of this length it is impossible to cover every aspect of that career in what was a preternaturally busy life, but most of his major projects as a conductor, composer and public music educator are covered in some detail. The private man will also be described, one whom his friends knew as loyal, generous, gregarious and witty, but a person who also fought demons that made his life difficult and messy. His inability to concentrate on a single aspect of his musical career placed him in a constant struggle between the desires to conduct and compose, and his outsized appetite for various pleasures – cigarettes, sex, food, alcohol and parties – surely compromised his health and probably shortened his life. Bernstein balanced his homosexuality with the need for a wife and family inculcated in him by his Jewish faith from a young age, an uneasy compromise that greatly complicated his relationship with the woman that he loved. His passions for various liberal causes and Israel were a large part of Bernstein's life, and figure prominently in this narrative. Perhaps the most fascinating thing about Bernstein was his all-embracing humanity, his desire to encounter and mingle with as many people and ideas as possible, an aspect of his personality that appears throughout this book.

1

'Safe at the Piano': Bernstein's Youth, 1918–39

Little in Leonard Bernstein's family background would have
indicated that he would become one of his generation's most
talented and prominent musicians.[1] Both of his parents were part
of the immigration of Ukrainian Jews fleeing pogroms and other
Russian restrictions on their lives in the decades around 1900. His
father, Shmuel Bernstein, son of an Orthodox rabbi, fled from his
village of Berezdov at the age of sixteen without telling his parents,
finally making his way to New York.[2] The man who became known
as Samuel Bernstein began his American life cleaning fish at the
Fulton Fish Market. Later he worked in his uncle's barbershop in
Hartford, Connecticut, entered the hair business as a supplier and
lived the American dream, starting the Samuel Bernstein Hair
Company and earning a comfortable income. His most fortunate
break came in the early 1920s when he became New England
distributor for an early permanent wave machine. In 1917 he married
Charna Resnick, whose family was from Shepetovka, Ukraine,
not far from Samuel's place of birth. When Charna was young her
family had moved to Poland; she came to the United States with
her mother in 1905, settling in Lawrence, Massachusetts, where her
father already worked in a textile mill. Known as 'Jennie', she was
fun-loving, poorly suited for the serious Samuel, who habitually
read the Talmud and quoted it often. He was moody and needed to
feel loved, and there were problems and separations early in their
marriage. Their unhappy union lasted until Samuel's death in 1969

and resulted in the birth of three children: Leonard (born 1918), Shirley (1923) and Burton (1932). Tension between Sam and Jenny was a regular feature of their family life, and the three children grew up with close relationships, especially Leonard and Shirley, but Burton also developed tight, lifelong associations with his older siblings.

Leonard Bernstein was born on 25 August 1918 in Lawrence, where Jenny had gone to be with her own family while giving birth. He was sickly and asthmatic, requiring careful care, but his natural intelligence manifested itself early as he was speaking well at about eighteen months. His legal, given name was 'Louis', after one of his mother's grandfathers and her younger brother, but his parents always called him 'Leonard', and Bernstein legally changed his name at the age of sixteen. He grew into a convincing composite of his parents: studious and religious like his father, occasionally suffering from dark moods, but also fun-loving and capable of great warmth like his mother, sharing her interest in films and other types of show business.

Bernstein craved music even as a young child, banging on a neighbour's door and calling for *moynik* (music), hoping that someone would play their piano. Jennie remembered that she could calm him with songs on the Victrola. Bernstein witnessed his father's enthusiasm for the right kind of music, seeing him dance exultantly in the Hasidic manner at parties. Jennie Bernstein also showed a love for music early in life when she wandered away from home and followed a *klezmer* band to another part of town.

In 1923 Samuel began to take his family to Mishkan Tefila Temple in Boston, the city's first Conservative synagogue, attended by many immigrant families who, like the Bernsteins, had begun to make their fortunes. It was there that the son began to attend Hebrew school at the age of eight and where he heard a live organ and choir for the first time under the direction of Solomon Gregory Braslavsky (1887–1975), an excellent musician who had left Vienna in 1928 to lead the temple's music. He was an important early influence on Bernstein and they stayed in touch for years.[3]

Bernstein's love for music found a personal focus in 1928 when his father's sister, Clara, moved to Brooklyn, leaving her brother's household with a sofa and an upright piano. Bernstein soon started to pick out tunes by ear and began lessons with Frieda Karp, a young woman in the neighbourhood who found her pupil rapidly moving on to Bach, Mendelssohn and Chopin. He surpassed her ability to help him and she recommended that Bernstein seek lessons at New England Conservatory. There he found Susan Williams, whose unorthodox ideas of piano technique held Bernstein back, but she also took him quickly into advanced literature by such composers as Paderewski, Brahms, Liszt and Beethoven.[4] He became interested in composing, writing multiple versions of pieces and asking his mother her preferences. His ability to play by ear developed as Bernstein worked out music that he heard on the radio.

Bernstein often practised on the grand piano at the home of his friend Mildred Spiegel, who encouraged him to audition for Heinrich Gebhard, one of Boston's leading piano teachers. Gebhard assigned Bernstein to his assistant Helen Coates, who became one of the most important figures in Bernstein's life. She taught him through high school, placing his lessons at the end of the day so that they could cover the large repertory that Bernstein was able to handle and so that she could help him notate his compositions. Just a year younger than Bernstein's mother, Coates recognized her student's talent and became devoted to him. When Bernstein's meteoric rise in the musical world began in 1944, she gave up her own career and became his secretary and confidante, a position she held until her death in 1989. Bernstein once said that he was 'safe at the piano',[5] and that feeling of security surely extended to his lessons with Helen Coates, who was probably as responsible as any person for helping Bernstein to find the discipline and focus that he needed to develop as a musician.

Bernstein's musical interests caused his father considerable consternation. He willingly paid for piano lessons at first but became angry when his son played the piano too late at night. Sam Bernstein's experience of musicians in Ukraine had been the poverty-stricken *klezmer* groups that played gigs for a few kopeks. He could not see music as a career possibility for his son, preferring that he succeed his father in the family business. As piano lessons became more expensive, Sam occasionally refused to pay for them, causing his son to earn money for lessons by teaching neighbourhood children or playing jazz and blues at parties with friends. The father did delight in his son's abilities, watching with pride as he played piano solos at temple meetings and on a cruise from Miami that father and son took together in the winter of 1932–3. He advertised his business on the radio in 1935, paying for a series of fifteen-minute programmes that featured the budding musician as piano soloist.[6] When his temple reserved a few tables at a Boston Pops concert in spring 1932, raising money for a Jewish charity in Palestine, Sam took Leonard and both sat transfixed by the finale, Ravel's *Bolero*. He paid for his son to attend some Boston Symphony Orchestra concerts and bought him the piano music for Gershwin's *Rhapsody in Blue* when Bernstein first heard the piece and fell in love with it, but he was not easily convinced that Leonard was destined for a musical career. On 14 May 1934 Bernstein played the first movement of Grieg's Piano Concerto in A minor with the Boston Public School Symphony Orchestra. His father skipped the concert, prompting Helen Coates to express her disappointment in a letter. His response expressed a father's satisfaction with Leonard's progress, but he noted that 'from a practical standpoint I prefer that he does not regard his music as a future means of maintenance.'[7] It should be noted, however, that Sam later paid for his son to attend Harvard for an academic music degree, a significant investment in his future.

Despite his father, young Bernstein pursued music with abandon. He taught Shirley the piano and together they read symphonic repertory in four hands and tackled scores for operas, covering both vocal parts and the piano accompaniment. Bernstein also found musical companionship outside the home, especially in the person of Sid Ramin, a neighbourhood boy just months younger than Bernstein who sometimes studied piano and theory with him, and they played piano duets. Ramin went on to a distinguished musical career as composer, arranger and conductor, aiding Bernstein as an orchestrator for such projects as *West Side Story* and *Mass*.[8]

Sam Bernstein's financial fortunes continued to grow even during the Depression, when people continued to have to get their hair styled. He built his family a small lakefront cottage in Sharon, Massachusetts. There Leonard first demonstrated his love for musical theatre, in 1934 and 1935 putting on neighbourhood productions of Bizet's *Carmen* and Gilbert and Sullivan's *The Mikado*, starring Bernstein, his sister and their friends, filled with local gags and satirical references to Jews and community life. The satire in *Carmen* even included female chorus members in *yarmulkes* and long beards, and the two leads were played by actors of the wrong gender, with Bernstein starring in the title role. His awareness of how his generation assimilated far more than that of his parents contributed to an artificial language called Rybernian that he created with his sister and friend Eddie Ryack. The language existed for private jokes and communication, but also to make fun of immigrant accents. The Bernstein siblings continued to speak Rybernian together throughout their lives.

Bernstein's education was in the Boston Public Schools. He graduated from sixth grade at the William Lloyd Garrison School in 1929 and then attended the prestigious Boston Latin School, where the rigorous curriculum – which included translating about forty lines of Latin every night – drove away two out of every three students who matriculated. Bernstein flourished and won awards in multiple academic areas, forging his formidable intellect. Six

The Boston Latin School, which Bernstein attended from 1929 to 1935.

years at Boston Latin in addition to his many musical activities and Hebrew studies kept Bernstein extremely busy throughout his adolescence, foreshadowing his later, frenetic professional life.

Bernstein at Harvard

Boston Latin sent many students on to Harvard College, including Leonard Bernstein in the autumn of 1935. He was a talented, cocksure young pianist seeking a liberal arts education and academic training as a music major. Performance at Harvard was strictly extracurricular, but there was a music faculty of renowned teachers and composers, including composer/theorist Walter Piston, composer Edward Burlingame Hill, musicologist A. Tillman Merritt and musicologist/composer Hugo Leichtentritt. Bernstein began to study the piano with Heinrich Gebhard, which Sam funded for all four years of his son's undergraduate work.

Harvard's Eliot House where Bernstein lived from 1936 to 1939.

Bernstein's self-confidence and irregular class attendance created challenges for the faculty, and he sometimes resented the exclusively academic nature of the training, but a curious musician like Bernstein could not help but be stimulated by such a brilliant faculty. What he might have sometimes lacked in dedication in a class he made up for with his intelligence and musicality, allowing him to wait until the last minute to do assignments but still succeed. Bernstein found a kindred spirit and major intellectual influence in philosophy professor David Prall, who taught a course in aesthetics and hosted discussions in his home that Bernstein frequented. Bernstein fell in love with Aaron Copland's Piano Variations; the professor bought him the sheet music and encouraged Bernstein to write a paper on it.[9] The young pianist memorized the piece and made it one of the more austere works in his repertory, which he insisted on playing at parties.

Bernstein wrote a senior honours thesis at Harvard entitled 'The Absorption of Race Elements into American Music', a document that he somehow completed in the midst of a blizzard of activities during his final year.[10] His central contention was that American composers had been influenced by music of Native Americans and African Americans since the 1890s, but nobody provided a true American voice until composers like Copland incorporated elements of jazz and blues. He further posited that the most effective examples of such absorption are pieces like Copland's Piano Variations, where one hears blues intervals and jazz rhythms embedded in modern musical structures. The strong opinions of this remarkable student document did not go over well with some on Harvard's faculty, but the thesis remained more or less intact.[11] In correspondence with Copland that year – how the two men met is described below – Bernstein described his intentions for his thesis and made it clear that he would stick to his ideas no matter what anyone said. The older, perhaps wiser Copland urged his young friend to try not to prove too much.[12] One can hear Bernstein's voice in this document and note ideas about the development of American music that he continued to espouse in later years.

Bernstein's extracurricular time at Harvard was remarkable for the many experiences that he crammed into it and contacts that he made with people who could assist his future career. His piano performances included three concertos with the Massachusetts State Symphony Orchestra, a Works Progress Administration (WPA)-sponsored ensemble and numerous duo recitals with Harold Shapero (1920–2013), a freshman when Bernstein was a junior who also became a noted composer. Their repertory included both classics and modern music, which Bernstein studied avidly, also accessing that knowledge in a memorable solo piano accompaniment to the silent film *Battleship Potemkin*, an effort applauded by the thousand students in the audience.[13] He completed several compositions during his college years, including a piano trio for his friend Mildred Spiegel and two of her colleagues, a set called Music for Two Pianos and a piano sonata, works that demonstrated his seriousness of purpose, catholicity of influences and dedication to his craft.[14] During his senior year he wrote incidental music for a performance of Aristophanes' *The Birds* in April 1939, a wildly eclectic score that helped bring the Greek satire into the modern era, including music that later appeared in several of Bernstein's mature works. *The Birds* was the first time that Bernstein conducted in public. His time at Harvard also saw him write music criticism, locally for the *Harvard Advocate* and nationally for the important New York-based journal *Modern Music*.[15] Bernstein did not spare his opinions, offering assessments that ranged from blunt to glowing, sometimes skewering works written by members of the Harvard faculty. Other important moments in Bernstein's life during his Harvard years took place in the summer of 1936, after his first year, when he produced *HMS Pinafore* in another of his Sharon local productions, and in the summer of 1937, which he spent as music counsellor at the all-Jewish Camp Onota in Pittsfield, Massachusetts, where he met Adolph Green, the lyricist who became a collaborator and lifelong friend.

What has been described thus far constitutes a worthwhile undergraduate experience, and one cannot underestimate the cachet of a Harvard degree for the bright young musician, but the connections that Bernstein made outside the classroom at Harvard had the most impact on his future. The first of these occurred in January 1937 when Bernstein attended a Boston Symphony Orchestra concert, witnessing the American debut of conductor Dimitri Mitropoulos (1896–1960). He met the Greek musician and played some of his compositions for him, impressing him with his musicality and future possibilities. Mitropoulos invited Bernstein to attend his rehearsals with the Boston Symphony. A passionate correspondence began and Bernstein spent a week with Mitropoulos in Minneapolis in April 1938. At one point he hoped to become his assistant at the Minneapolis Symphony Orchestra, but this proved impossible.[16] Bernstein was profoundly influenced by Mitropoulos's demonstrative conducting and playing of piano concertos while conducting from the keyboard.

After attending a dance performance by Anna Sokolow in Boston, Bernstein decided to attend her New York debut with a graduate student friend. It took place at the Guild Theater on 14 November 1937, and by chance the nineteen-year-old Bernstein found himself sitting next to Aaron Copland (1900–1990), composer of the beloved Piano Variations. It was Copland's birthday, and he invited the young musician back to his loft for the party. Never shy, Bernstein played the Piano Variations for the composer and

Symphony Hall, the home of the Boston Symphony Orchestra, where Bernstein first heard an orchestra, and where he later occasionally guest conducted.

clearly impressed him. They became friends (and probably more), corresponding often and seeing each other when possible. Copland, for example, attended *The Birds* in Cambridge in April 1939 and saw Bernstein conduct, inspiring him to advise the younger musician to seek training in the discipline. Bernstein showed his compositions to Copland, who commented on his work and urged him to find *la note choisie*, or 'the chosen note' that raises a chord or passage beyond the ordinary, an important part of Copland's training from Nadia Boulanger in the early 1920s.[17] Bernstein later stated that this was the closest thing he ever had to real training in composition. Thus was initiated a lifelong friendship that was to have a remarkable influence on the careers of both men.

This procession of famous musical figures entering the young Bernstein's life while a student at Harvard was not over. The left-leaning young pianist was fascinated by the excitement surrounding Marc Blitzstein's *The Cradle Will Rock* – a paean to the labour movement and strong condemnation of capitalism – in its storied, controversial 1937 premiere. Barred from their own theatre by the Federal Theatre Project, part of President Roosevelt's New Deal, and under threat from Congressional Republicans, Blitzstein (1905–1964) played the score on the piano as the only figure on stage at the Venice Theatre while actors performed their parts from the audience. Bernstein convinced the Harvard Dramatic Club to produce the work on 5 May 1939, and he was involved in many aspects of the effort. Faculty sponsors included Archibald MacLeish, Arthur Schlesinger Sr and David Prall.[18] Demonstrating his talent for self-promotion – many might have called it *chutzpah* – Bernstein invited the composer to the performance. Blitzstein was impressed and spent hours in conversation with the college senior in a long walk along the Charles River, beginning another intense, lifelong friendship. Blitzstein described Bernstein at the time as a reincarnation of his own personage.[19] As Allen Shawn has noted, after Copland, Blitzstein became one of Bernstein's most profound influences as a composer, especially in the way that the older composer set the English language to music.[20]

Beyond his educational and early professional accomplishments, Bernstein's mature personality was becoming clear. Reared in a home by parents who leaned to the left politically, Bernstein was at Harvard at a time when American liberalism was riding high with the New Deal. There were many Marxists at Harvard, and Bernstein's own politics flowed far to the left, as may be seen in his production of *The Cradle Will Rock*, an event that brought him to the attention of Cambridge police who were investigating Communist activities at Harvard. It was also at this time that an informant denounced Bernstein to the FBI, which started a file on him.[21] Copland and Blitzstein both would have influenced Bernstein to seek more connection with those who espoused Marxism. In addition both older composers were homosexuals, as was Mitropoulos. Sexual relationships between men, especially those pursued at a time when homosexuality was treated as a mental disorder, are difficult to establish with certainty, but the young Bernstein certainly had the opportunity to be intimate with each of these men. Various writings by Bernstein surviving from high school and college demonstrate that he was wrestling with his own sexuality and pursued relationships with both men and women.[22] Joan Peyser has argued that Bernstein's 'powerful sexuality' was perhaps the most important part of his character, and his extant letters demonstrate that it was a significant part of his life.[23] Meetings and friendships that he started with Mitropoulos, Copland and Blitzstein before his 21st birthday had a profound influence on his development as a musician and a man, helping to set up the next four years of his life when he found his genius as a conductor and took the steps that would quickly make him famous.

2

'The Spirit of Koussevitzky':
Bernstein Discovers Conducting,
1939—43

Looking back on Bernstein's career with hindsight makes it seem
as though he marched inevitably from one success to another, and
during the four years following his graduation Bernstein completed
his musical training and did some work in the field, but there would
have been plenty of moments between June 1939 and August 1943
when this ambitious young man probably felt that success would
never come his way.[1] His father offered him a job in the family
business at $100 per week after he graduated. Considering he could
live at home for nothing, it was a lucrative possibility, but Bernstein
went to New York City for the summer to see what work he might
find, an impossible task given the fact that the musicians' union had
a six-month residency requirement. Bernstein shared an apartment
with Adolph Green while hanging out with his improvisation group
The Revuers (which included Betty Comden, who became one of
Bernstein's best friends) at the Village Vanguard in Greenwich
Village and playing the piano for them, looking for work and
composing while showing his efforts to Copland for criticism.
It was during the summer of 1939 that he began work on his
Symphony no. 1, 'Jeremiah', at that time working on the third
movement, originally an independent piece for mezzo-soprano
and orchestra.

Bernstein had been shown the possibility of a career as a
conductor by Mitropoulos, and Copland also recognized his innate
ability. Bernstein started to take this possibility seriously during this

summer of relative inactivity, hoping that some of his well-placed friends might help him find a fellowship at Juilliard for the autumn, but this proved impossible. Copland thought that Bernstein should consider the Curtis Institute of Music in Philadelphia, supplying him with a ticket so that he could attend a concert that Curtis conducting professor Fritz Reiner was leading at Lewisohn Stadium and advising how to meet him backstage. Bernstein did, and Reiner suggested that he audition in September.[2] Bernstein returned to Boston early that month. At that point Mitropoulos seemed to reappear miraculously after meeting some of Bernstein's friends on an Atlantic crossing, telling them that Bernstein should find him at the Hotel Biltmore in New York City. The conductor told his protégé that his future was conducting and he would help him get into Curtis.[3] At his audition, Reiner, then conductor of the Pittsburgh Symphony Orchestra, put Bernstein through his paces. After demonstrating his prodigious sight-reading ability from an orchestral score at the piano and answering questions, Bernstein was accepted into Reiner's class at this, one of the country's leading music schools. In addition to working with Reiner, Bernstein enrolled in the piano studio of Isabelle Vengerova, a stern Russian pedagogue who instilled more discipline into the free-wheeling young pianist and helped him to finish the development of his professional technique.

By musical standards, at 21 Bernstein was not young to begin his first real training in a music school. Four years at Harvard had allowed him to grow intellectually and he pursued many extracurricular performance possibilities, but at Curtis he was thrown into an intensive, structured experience where he was among the older students. Like Vengerova, Reiner was a strict taskmaster who demanded complete preparation from his students. Simply knowing how to beat time through a score was not sufficient. He expected a student to know what note each instrument was playing at any given moment and to have an analytical knowledge of a work's form, stylistic construction and expressive markings. Reiner was apparently humourless with his students – Bernstein called him 'mean'[4] – and possessed a cutting wit that he applied mercilessly, perhaps exactly what Bernstein needed because he had much to learn and large deficits in musical discipline and repertory. It could not have been easy for one as wilful and self-assured as Bernstein, but his explosion on the musical scene only two years after he left Curtis shows that he made good use of his time there. At the end of his first semester, Bernstein was the only conducting student to receive an A from Reiner.[5] While at Curtis, Bernstein also studied score-reading with Renée Longy-Miquelle (who became a very good friend and apparently for a time his lover[6]) and orchestration with distinguished composer Randall Thompson, the school's director.

Outside of excelling in his studies, Bernstein's two years in Philadelphia were not easy. His father either gave him a small

The Curtis Institute of Music in Philadelphia, where Bernstein studied conducting and piano from 1939 to 1941.

allowance or nothing at all and Mitropoulos supplemented his income with regular gifts.[7] He was the only university graduate studying at Curtis, and his cocky manner and great talent made him unpopular with his peers. Bernstein later said that another conducting student who could not sight-read scores nearly as well once boasted that he had a gun and planned to shoot Bernstein, Reiner and Thompson; apparently the police were called and the man was escorted away.[8] In the winter of 1940 Mitropoulos wrote to Bernstein with the proposal that he come to Minneapolis for the 1940–41 season to play the piano in the orchestra, attend all rehearsals with scores in hand and conduct the orchestra in rehearsals. Bernstein fervently desired that this might come to pass, but in the end the conductor could not arrange it with the local union or orchestral manager.[9] The disappointed Bernstein wrote to his friend composer David Diamond on 18 April, regretting that 'every move, every score studied, project rejected, person loved, hope ignored, was a direct preparation for next year. From the scores I chose to study to the sexual life which I have abandoned – all.'[10] For Bernstein, work at Curtis was just that; he appears to have curbed at least some of his voracious sexual appetite as he studied his conducting and practised the piano extensively. On 7 February 1941, about the middle of his second year, Bernstein wrote to his Boston friend Mildred Spiegel and compared the remainder of his time at Curtis to finishing a jail sentence.[11] He also regularly wrote to her with pride about his successes in conducting and piano performances, meaning that Bernstein understood why he was at Curtis.

However satisfying Bernstein might have found his performances at Curtis, he was profoundly interested when he heard that the Boston Symphony Orchestra and its famed conductor Sergei Koussevitzky (1874–1951) were starting the Berkshire Music Festival in the summer of 1940, where conducting students would be able to work with a student orchestra. He immediately applied and organized recommendations from Reiner and other prominent friends. Home in Boston in March, Bernstein attended a Boston Symphony Orchestra concert and went backstage afterwards to meet Koussevitzky, who accepted him as a Tanglewood conducting student. In the distinguished Russian conductor the young man found his most important mentor. Koussevitzky had begun his career as a virtuoso double bassist. After marrying into a wealthy family, he founded his own orchestra that performed in Moscow and St Petersburg, and later he led his own orchestra in Paris. Koussevitzky conducted the Boston Symphony Orchestra from 1924 to 1949, continuing his generous commissioning of pieces from contemporary composers and leading many premieres. The American composer with whom he became most closely associated was Copland, who taught composition at the first Berkshire Music Festival. During his Boston career, Koussevitzky conducted eleven works by the American composer, including five premieres.[12] Copland's respect for Koussevitzky would have been communicated to Bernstein, who also had seen him conduct a number of Boston Symphony Orchestra concerts, once expressing his great envy of the man to Mildred Spiegel at a Symphony Hall concert.[13] As the conductor of Bernstein's hometown orchestra, a striking and flamboyant figure, and one of the most important supporters and interpreters of modern symphonic music, Koussevitzky came to represent for Bernstein many of the things that he hoped to be himself. When the Russian conductor identified Bernstein as his favourite student and protégé, the young musician was ready for the load of expectations and made Koussevitzky his hero. On inheriting his cufflinks after his death, Bernstein never led a concert without wearing them. Bernstein also imitated the way that the older musician walked and wore his clothes. His later dedication to Brandeis University, Tanglewood and teaching conducting were all based on his love for Koussevitzky.

Founding the Berkshire Music Festival was one of Koussevitzky's visionary efforts. He assembled a first-class faculty and for the initial

Serge Koussevitzky (1874–1951), conductor of the Boston Symphony Orchestra, 1924–49, and Bernstein's most important mentor as a conductor.

summer drew three hundred students. The centre of the experience for Bernstein was the maestro's advanced class in conducting, which included, in addition to Bernstein, Richard Bales, Lukas Foss, Thor Johnson and Gaylord Browne.[14] At a time when few American conductors enjoyed any fame, these five students had the opportunity to lead the student orchestra at Tanglewood each week. In the six weeks Bernstein performed the following with the 66-member Institute Orchestra: Randall Thompson's Symphony no. 2, J. S. Bach's Double Violin Concerto, the second and fourth movements of Rimsky-Korsakov's *Scheherazade*, a *Sinfonia Concertante* by Haydn, Brahms's Variations on a Theme by Haydn, Copland's *An Outdoor Overture* and Stravinsky's *L'Histoire du soldat* with a smaller ensemble and his own comic text.[15] It was an extraordinary summer for a young conducting student. The Second World War raged in Europe and Asia, but Bernstein spent July and August 1940 feeling as though he had found his place in the world under the watchful eye of a man whom both considered Bernstein's surrogate father. Speaking to Tanglewood students in 1970, Bernstein described the wonderful experiences of the early festivals, imputing it all to 'the spirit of Koussevitzky'.[16]

Koussevitzky did not want Bernstein to return for his second year at Curtis, telling his student that all he needed was a three-year course with him and he would become one of the great conductors. Bernstein was keen to accept Koussevitzky's offer and tried to explain his reasoning in a letter to Reiner, but the Hungarian conductor and his institution were not about to give up one of their star pupils. Reiner had originally told Bernstein that he could not return to Curtis if he spent the summer with Koussevitzky – even though he wrote his student a letter of recommendation – but Curtis director Randall Thompson felt differently and brokered a deal involving the two conductors and future relations between Curtis and Tanglewood.[17] Bernstein returned for his second year at Curtis with a generous, monthly no-term loan from the school and free lunches.

Bernstein must have attended to his studies brilliantly that year because he earned his diploma in May with sterling grades, and the academic year of 1940–41 saw the blizzard of activity that became his wont. Bernstein's name appeared for the first time on a musical publication: a piano transcription of Copland's *El salón México*. Copland arranged for Boosey & Hawkes to pay Bernstein $25 for the work, but in a letter of 16 December 1940 he promised his protégé a long lecture when he discovered that Bernstein had no idea how to prepare a manuscript for publication.[18] Bernstein sought part-time employment that year, teaching piano at a private boys' school and directing a chorus. He also orchestrated a ballet for composer Paul

Bowles, whom Bernstein had met through Copland several years before, and played the piano on radio performances that Helen Coates heard back in Boston.[19] He had a steady girlfriend that year in Philadelphia, Shirley Gabis, a sixteen-year-old piano student who became a lifelong friend, but Bernstein also reported on men that he was seeing in letters to Copland. His ambivalence about Gabis showed when he wrote to Copland sometime in January 1941: 'Saw my 16-yr-old girl – I don't know.'[20] He ended his year at Curtis triumphantly with a broadcast performance of Brahms's Serenade in A major with the Curtis Orchestra and in performances in a recital by Vengerova's graduating pupils, where he played Scriabin's Piano Sonata no. 5 and two movements from Ravel's *Le Tombeau de Couperin*. Bernstein even found time to work on his own violin sonata that year, a work inspired by his friend violinist Raphael Hillyer (later founding violist in the Juilliard Quartet), but the sonata was not published during Bernstein's lifetime. After graduating from Curtis, he rushed to Boston to put the finishing touches to his incidental score to Aristophanes' *The Peace*, another effort for the Harvard Student Union. All of this occurred in the uncertainty that pervades a time when war threatens: Bernstein had registered for the possible draft in the autumn of 1940.

Bernstein's return to the Berkshire Music Festival during July and August 1941 was a foregone conclusion. While waiting for it to start in June, Bernstein won an opportunity to conduct the Boston Pops at an Esplanade concert through a *Boston Herald* music quiz. On 11 June he conducted Wagner's Prelude to *Die Meistersinger* before a large crowd. At Tanglewood he was again the star student in Koussevitzky's advanced conducting class and led the Institute Orchestra in three works: William Schuman's *American Festival Overture*, Constant Lambert's *The Rio Grande* (Bernstein's first experience with chorus and orchestra) and Brahms's Piano Concerto no. 2 with Carlos Moseley as the soloist, a man who later became significant to Bernstein as managing director of the New York

Philharmonic. Bernstein's other main performance that summer was as the pianist in Copland's *Vitebsk (Study on a Jewish Theme)*.[21]

Copland was again on the compositional faculty at Tanglewood, but Bernstein's romantic intentions that summer seemed to have been directed at Jacqueline 'Kiki' Speyer, the attractive daughter of a Boston Symphony Orchestra musician that Bernstein had met the previous summer and already dated. Reportedly Koussevitzky pushed Bernstein towards her as well.[22] The conductor felt that members of his profession needed to wield moral and musical authority, and his conventional view would not have included Bernstein's active sex life with members of both sexes. Things apparently progressed far with Speyer. Sometime in August 1941 he boarded a train for Key West, Florida, noting in a letter to Shirley Gabis that he was away for 'a week of escape', later cryptically stating that he was running away from Kiki Speyer.[23] Later that autumn, Bernstein wrote to Copland and stated that he had explained 'the whole summer fiasco' to Speyer – apparently admitting his homosexuality – but 'she wants to marry me anyway, and accept the double life, or try for my recovery. And Alex blows in on all this! It's such a confused week!'[24] Even as he contemplated marriage, Bernstein appears to have been seeing a male paramour. Bernstein reported to Copland in a letter from early 1942 that Speyer had given up on him as a potential mate.[25] She wrote to Bernstein to offer best wishes with his teaching studio and that she was confident of his ultimate success. Her postscript perhaps spoke volumes: 'That has killed the bad taste . . . so chalk it up as your first fan letter.'[26] Meryle Secrest interviewed Speyer for her Bernstein biography. She stated how closely attached Speyer was to Bernstein in the summer of 1941 and how often they discussed marriage, but Bernstein allowed Speyer to catch him after he had spent the night with a man and had her tell Koussevitzky of his homosexuality. Speyer realized that she could never control Bernstein, which she believes is what Koussevitzky had hoped.[27]

Kiki Speyer's confidence in Bernstein's success underlined the bitter truth of his life in 1941–2: he was a supremely talented musician but also a young American conductor looking for his first job. Even with all of his famous friends, it would not prove simple for Bernstein to solve this conundrum. Still, from a distance of more than seventy years and considering the difficulty that most people experience in trying to launch a career in the arts, Bernstein's two years before he became assistant conductor of the New York Philharmonic in August 1943 does not seem like too much suffering. It should also be acknowledged that, although Bernstein was frustrated with his lack of opportunities during this time, his musical activities were not interrupted by a non-musical job. During this period he wrote both his clarinet sonata and his first symphony, works that contributed to his early success as a composer.

Also, given the fact that the United States began its largest military mobilization in late 1941, it seems extraordinarily fortunate that Bernstein was able to launch his career at all during the Second World War. His 4F status because of asthma – making him permanently ineligible for the draft – was gradually clarified, and Bernstein's letters show that he welcomed the dispensation. He wrote to Koussevitzky in triumph in August 1943, stating that a doctor had examined him while he was suffering from asthmatic hay fever and that the physician was 'a firm believer in the British policy of leaving as intact as possible the cultural foundations of our country, even – or rather especially – in time of war'.[28] With a medical excuse, Bernstein felt 'no guilt' regarding his deferment.

Bernstein remained in the Boston area, supported by his father, until after Tanglewood in 1942. His father helped him rent a studio and print cards announcing his availability as a teacher of piano and musical analysis, but this was just before Pearl Harbor; he found only one student. Although little of this activity would have resulted in appreciable income, Bernstein did perform in several capacities as a pianist, including in a duet recital with Harold Shapero for the New York League of Composers in February and numerous appearances in April with singer Eric Stein at the Fox and Hounds nightclub in Boston performing songs they wrote together.[29]

Bernstein organized three concerts at Boston's Institute of Modern Art that spring: another duet recital with Shapero, a programme featuring the premiere of Bernstein's Sonata for Clarinet and Piano and a production of Copland's opera *The Second Hurricane*. Bernstein spent a few idyllic days with Copland at his summer cottage before Tanglewood started. It was a disappointing season because with the war and transportation restrictions the Boston Symphony Orchestra pulled out, but Koussevitzky forged ahead, conducting the better student orchestra. Bernstein was his assistant, but he was left with leading a second orchestra of disappointing quality. After that summer, Koussevitzky mothballed the Berkshire Music Festival for the duration of the war. Certainly a joy for Bernstein that year was meeting clarinettist David Oppenheim, one of his major love interests into the next year and a close, lifelong friend. Aspects of their relationship appear in their extant correspondence, such as their feelings about Marketa Morris ('The Frau'), the German analyst with whom both were working, partly on trying to end their homosexual urges.[30] Other letters, especially those to Copland, seem to illustrate that Bernstein's active pursuit of sexual experiences was unlikely to be curbed by an analyst.[31]

Bernstein's major compositional effort from 1941–2 was the Sonata for Clarinet and Piano. Oppenheim played the New York premiere with Bernstein in a League of Composers concert on 14 March 1943, and they recorded it. The sonata was Bernstein's first published composition. Allen Shawn has commented that the composer perhaps undervalued his Sonata for Violin and Piano (segments of which later became part of the ballet *Facsimile* and Symphony no. 2), which was unpublished until after his death, but Bernstein clearly believed his work for clarinet and piano to be a worthy effort.[32] While not a completely mature work, with segments more than a bit reminiscent of Hindemith and Copland, and all of it packed into about ten short minutes, the work demonstrates Bernstein's bent for melodic display and irresistible rhythmic elan, especially in the 5/8 portion of the last movement. The evocative first movement is one of Bernstein's most carefully drawn sonata forms, and the opening portion of the second movement is thoughtful and pleading, entering the quintuple metre without break, where one starts to hear hints of Bernstein the theatrical composer. Copland found his protégé's music too derivative, writing to Bernstein about the clarinet sonata on 25 March 1943: 'It's still full of Hindemith, because I say so . . . I want to hear about your writing a song that has no Copland, no Hindemith, no Strauss, no Bloch, no Milhaud and no Bartók. Then I'll talk to you.'[33] Bernstein had recently told his mentor about one of his new works that sounded like the older composer's music.

After Tanglewood in 1942, Bernstein closed his Boston studio and moved to New York City, living, among other places, in the basement of the Park Savoy Hotel for $8 per week. He played performances with The Revuers that autumn, also coaching singers and playing the piano for dance classes in Carnegie Hall, but found regular employment with Harms-Witmark, a music publisher. Although Bernstein wrote to Koussevitzky on 29 May 1943 describing his 'horrible chores' that were 'dull beyond belief', surely he learned worthwhile things related to his future composition of theatrical music while transcribing jazz solos and making two- and four-hand transcriptions of popular songs.[34] Bernstein published these efforts under the pseudonym 'Lenny Amber', the latter the English for 'Bernstein'.

In late 1942 Bernstein finished his Symphony no. 1, 'Jeremiah', in response to a competition contest at New England Conservatory; Koussevitzky was head of the jury. Bernstein finished writing out the orchestral score with help from his sister and several friends, and took a train to Boston with Edys Merrill, his current apartment

mate, so that she could turn the score in for him anonymously
at the deadline on 31 December. Although the symphony failed to
win, Bernstein's employer Harms agreed to publish it. Bernstein
sent the score to Reiner and Koussevitzky, who apparently remained
in competition over Bernstein, with the result that the young
musician would conduct the Pittsburgh Symphony Orchestra in
the work's premiere in January 1944 and in Boston the following
month. The 'Jeremiah' is an impressive first symphony. The third
movement is the setting from the Lamentations of Jeremiah that
Bernstein had written in 1939 for mezzo-soprano and orchestra.
In the autumn of 1942 he added two introductory movements,
'Prophecy' and 'Profanation', forming a programme concerning
the prophet's predictions about the fall of Jerusalem to the
Babylonians in 586 BCE, a description of the sins of the Jewish
people and the final lament. Bernstein used cantillation melodies
from Jewish worship in each movement, including, for example,
the opening horn melody in 'Prophecy', combining the declamatory
feeling one hears in Copland with frank lyricism that is less
common in the older composer.[35] For 'Profanation' Bernstein
provided a sort of modern party music with the shifting metres
and unpredictable groups of two and three quavers (eighth notes)
that one often hears in Copland and Stravinsky, but also elements
of Broadway music that later would have been comfortable in *West
Side Story*. 'Lamentation' is lyrical and profoundly Jewish in tone,
somewhat like the music of Ernest Bloch, but it is highly effective
and the first indication of Bernstein's gift for vocal writing. Bernstein
dedicated the symphony to his father, the most important Jewish
influence in his life. The work takes on a special poignancy when
one considers that Bernstein wrote it during the Holocaust, a
disastrous event for Bernstein's family and so many others who
had relatives in areas ruled by the Nazis. Minor works that Bernstein
wrote at about this time were the song cycle *I Hate Music!*, the title
of which came from comments made by roommate Edys Merrill,

and five *Anniversaries* for solo piano dedicated to friends and mentors, a type of piano miniature that he returned to a number of times in his career.

The year 1943 brought plenty of signs that Bernstein was perceived as an effective pianist and conductor. Copland found himself unable to return from California, where he was working on a film score, to play his Piano Sonata at a Town Hall event in February that included a discussion forum on the piece. Bernstein substituted for him with little warning and also impressed the audience when he spoke at the forum. Bernstein made his New York conducting debut on 30 March in a performance of Paul Bowles's opera *The Wind Remains* at the Museum of Modern Art. By this point, Bernstein had been noticed by Artur Rodzinski, who had been appointed the new director of the New York Philharmonic starting that autumn. In a letter to Oppenheim on 5 March Bernstein stated that Bruno Zirato, assistant manager of the orchestra, had called to tell him of the conductor's interest in hiring Bernstein as assistant conductor.[36] He learned for certain of his new position at Rodzinski's summer home in Stockbridge, Massachusetts, on his 25th birthday, 25 August 1943. He was on his way, and fame was just around the corner.

3

'I have a fine large apartment in Carnegie Hall': A Time of Searching, 1943–51

The new position in which Leonard Bernstein found himself, with its advantageously placed lodgings, must have seemed like a dream come true.[1] He was trying to carve out a symphonic career when there were few successful American conductors of any age, let alone those who, like Bernstein, pursued their training in the United States. European study had for decades been de rigueur for leading American figures in classical music; given the approach of war, however, it would have been difficult for Bernstein to have studied in Europe. He was also handicapped by his Jewish identity. Jews in the United States had made major strides in theatre and film in the first half of the twentieth century, but leading American positions in classical music were often occupied by Europeans who either were not born Jewish or who had converted, such as Koussevitzky, who once suggested to Bernstein that he would have a better chance for success by changing his name to something that sounded less Jewish. Koussevitzky suggested 'Leonard S. Burns' ('S' for Samuelovich, or 'son of Samuel'), but Bernstein declined.

Bernstein's new duties included learning all of the scores that the Philharmonic played under Rodzinski or a guest conductor so that he might substitute as needed and to peruse new works that composers submitted to the Philharmonic. Bernstein's reward for all of this work was a chance to conduct the ensemble in a concert at Carnegie Hall late in the season. It had been many years since an assistant conductor had actually filled in for an indisposed maestro in a major programme.

Fortune smiled on Bernstein in several areas; he was simply not destined to remain an anonymous assistant conductor for long. He continued to compose part-time, as was to be the case for most of his life. He had met the Russian mezzo-soprano Jennie Tourel; they became friends, and she scheduled his song cycle *I Hate Music* on her debut New York recital, scheduled for Town Hall on 13 November, and they had already performed the set in Lenox, Massachusetts in August. Bernstein invited his family to the New York premiere and they attended, not knowing that their son had already heard that guest conductor Bruno Walter had the flu and might have to miss the afternoon matinee performance the next day. Following the recital, Bernstein stayed most of the night at the party at Tourel's apartment, only to be wakened the next morning at 9 a.m. to hear that Rodzinski had declined to come into the city and substitute for Walter, so Bernstein would be leading the nationally broadcast performance that afternoon. He called his parents and told them to stay in town and sit in the conductor's box for the performance, and then went to speak to Walter about moments to watch out for in the scores, which included Robert Schumann's 'Manfred' Overture, Miklós Rósza's *Theme, Variations and Finale*, Richard Strauss's *Don Quixote* and Richard Wagner's prelude to *Die Meistersinger*. It was a tricky programme that would have benefited from rehearsal time, especially the Strauss, a complicated tone poem with major solo parts for a cellist and a violist, and Rósza's piece included many rhythmic difficulties. Bernstein, however, went on cold, knowing that the first three pieces would be broadcast nationwide. The concert went remarkably well, with many curtain calls for the young conductor. At intermission and afterwards in the green room his parents were effusive, his father surely surprised by this turn of events.

The programme of Bernstein's debut with the New York Philharmonic on 14 November 1943, when he substituted for Bruno Walter with no rehearsal.

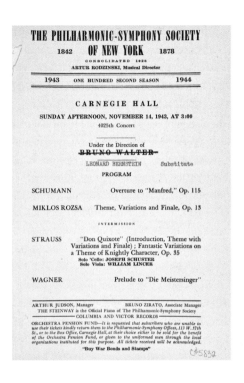

THE PHILHARMONIC-SYMPHONY SOCIETY
1842   OF NEW YORK   1878
CONSOLIDATED 1928
ARTUR RODZINSKI, Musical Director

1943   ONE HUNDRED SECOND SEASON   1944

CARNEGIE HALL

SUNDAY AFTERNOON, NOVEMBER 14, 1943, AT 3:00
4025th Concert

Under the Direction of
~~BRUNO WALTER~~

LEONARD BERNSTEIN   Substitute

PROGRAM

SCHUMANN   Overture to "Manfred", Op. 115

MIKLOS ROZSA   Theme, Variations and Finale, Op. 13

INTERMISSION

STRAUSS   "Don Quixote" (Introduction, Theme with
               Variations and Finale) ; Fantastic Variations on
               a Theme of Knightly Character, Op. 35
               Solo 'Cello: JOSEPH SCHUSTER
               Solo Viola: WILLIAM LINCER

WAGNER   Prelude to "Die Meistersinger"

ARTHUR JUDSON, Manager   BRUNO ZIRATO, Associate Manager
THE STEINWAY is the Official Piano of The Philharmonic-Symphony Society
COLUMBIA AND VICTOR RECORDS
ORCHESTRA PENSION FUND—It is requested that subscribers who are unable to
use their tickets kindly return them to the Philharmonic-Symphony Offices, 113 W. 57th
St., or to the Box Office, Carnegie Hall, at their choice either to be sold for the benefit
of the Orchestra Pension Fund, or given to the uniformed men through the local
organizations instituted for this purpose. All tickets received will be acknowledged.
"Buy War Bonds and Stamps"

In a wartime city and nation looking for good news, Bernstein quickly became a media sensation. His success was a front-page story in the *New York Times* the next day, and in another article music critic Olin Downes praised Bernstein's work, also including this prescient remark: 'Mr. Bernstein, on the occasion of the first public concert he ever conducted with a major symphony, showed that he is one of the very few conductors of the rising generation who are indubitably to be reckoned with.'[2] The *Daily News* applied a baseball metaphor, comparing Bernstein to an outfielder making a dangerous shoestring catch.[3] It was the beginning of the blizzard of publicity that was to accompany Bernstein's life, a constant stream of highlights that the musician clearly enjoyed, but that also provided significant challenges. Both Bernstein and his family

– who could never have been prepared for the many interviews that followed – made unfortunate statements. To one reporter Bernstein said, 'I look like a well-built dope fiend,' a humorous self-assessment that plagued him for years.[4] His father found himself fending off charges that he had discouraged his son's musical career, stating, 'How could I know my son would grow up to be Leonard Bernstein?'[5]

The memorable year continued. Bernstein had already been scheduled to lead Ernest Bloch's *Three Jewish Poems* in a broadcast concert the next Sunday, and two weeks later he substituted for American conductor Harold Barlow, who was ill, this time with one rehearsal. The result was another success in a programme of Delius, Brahms and Beethoven. Rodzinski, becoming increasingly angry over his assistant's fame, once grabbed Bernstein by the collar.[6]

Just as Bernstein became one of the few famous young conductors in the United States, his first symphony became known. The 'Jeremiah' triumphed in both Pittsburgh and Boston that winter (Bernstein's first significant guest conducting with major orchestras; later that spring he filled in for another ailing conductor in Montreal), and then Rodzinski allowed the composer to conduct his symphony with the New York Philharmonic four times in March and April. It won the New York Music Critics Circle award that May as the best new classical composition and was heard in a national broadcast by the NBC Symphony Orchestra under Frank Rich. To have such sudden success as a young conductor and composer was, to say the least, unusual.

Fancy Free and *On the Town*

Bernstein was working on another memorable premiere. In the autumn he had met the young dancer Jerome Robbins, soloist with the Ballet Theatre. For his debut as a choreographer Robbins had sold his company on a scenario involving high-spirited sailors on leave in New York City. It was a fresh idea that required a composer who could provide music with jazz and blues tropes. Robbins's search brought him to Bernstein, who demonstrated that he had the right musical touch. Robbins arranged a commission from the Ballet Theatre for the paltry sum of $300.[7]

Working together was a challenge. Robbins was on the road for much of the winter and Bernstein was busy. He loved the stimulation of live collaboration, and there were times when he worked with Robbins and another dancer in a studio, improvising while they choreographed, but most of the time he composed alone, making recordings on two pianos with Copland that Bernstein sent to Robbins along with sections of the score. A number of his letters to Robbins survive, demonstrating details and the spirit of their work.

Bernstein often struggled to find time to compose, but he made *Fancy Free* a priority. In a letter of December 1943 he suggested having a song in a popular style sung from the stage,[8] but ultimately they used a recording of 'Big Stuff', a bluesy song by Bernstein recorded by his sister. Bernstein found himself writing extensively for solo piano, a characteristic way to represent jazz and blues, but he was concerned with how well solo piano would be heard in the Metropolitan Opera House.[9] Robbins pressed Bernstein to keep the music, especially rhythms, as simple as possible; the composer protested that he was doing so, but he clearly wanted the rhythms to be interesting. He told Robbins to add bars or repeats where necessary, but also wanted to avoid the music becoming boring.[10] Bernstein provided musical descriptions for specific actions (often called 'Mickey-Mousing', commonly heard in animation underscoring), such as the sailors splitting a piece of chewing gum.[11] At one point Bernstein suggested that perhaps the scoring should be for just two pianos and percussion,[12] but Robbins apparently wanted a full orchestra. Bernstein defended his work in terms of affect, once averring to Robbins that Variation 2 is not 'melancholy', calling it 'whimsical, *very dancy*, a little poignant in the harmony, full of lyrical jazziness.'[13]

The ballet includes seven major sections: 'Enter Three Sailors', 'Scene at a Bar', 'Enter Two Girls', 'Pas de deux', 'Competition Scene', 'Three Dance Variations' ('Galop', 'Waltz', 'Danzon' [*sic*]) and 'Finale'. Jazz and Latin references permeate the first three sections with block-scoring in the winds like one hears in big bands, solo piano, rumba rhythms and percussion effects reminiscent of a trap set. In 'Enter Two Girls' there are horn fanfares like those in the second movement of Rimsky-Korsakov's *Scheherazade*. The 'Pas de deux' is more inspired by blues, with effective scoring for solo winds. 'Competition Scene' is a mixture of jazz references and the influences of Stravinsky's *Petrushka* and more *Scheherazade*, while 'Galop' and 'Waltz' are neoclassical takes on those European dance types with blues references and swinging dotted rhythms in the latter section. The 'Danzon' is one of Bernstein's first Latin-inspired movements, perhaps influenced by Copland's *Danzón cubano*, completed in 1942. (Bernstein played the premiere of the two-piano version with Copland.) Several of the ballet's previous musical ideas come together to form the 'Finale'.

Fancy Free was a hit. Celebrating American sailors during the war was good box office, and Robbins, who danced one of the roles, effectively balanced movements from social dances with balletic athleticism and artistic sensibilities. The sailors are confident, exhibiting exuberant swagger and a sense of companionship, but desperate enough for female attention to fight with each other when there are too few women in the bar. The women leave, enjoying their power over the men. With Bernstein conducting, he had the opportunity to communicate his sense of the music and set the tempos. Impresario Sol Hurok had to extend the season by two weeks with standing-room-only crowds, and the work toured. Bernstein had found a like-minded collaborator, and extended his compositional reach into the dance world.

Making *Fancy Free* into a musical was suggested by Oliver Smith, a theatrical designer who had worked on both the ballet and *On the Town*; Smith produced the show with Paul Feigay.[14] Bernstein insisted on bringing Betty Comden and Adolph Green into the project for lyrics and the book, the latter referring to the remainder of the show, including dialogue and stage directions. They worked together in the second half of 1944 in such places as a Manhattan hospital in June where Bernstein and Green each had minor surgery, and in southern California in August where Robbins and Bernstein were on tour with *Fancy Free*. They carefully used songs and dance sequences in service of plot and characterization, the latest goal for progressive creators of Broadway musicals, as realized brilliantly by Richard Rodgers and Oscar Hammerstein II in *Oklahoma!* (1943). Robbins devised more ballet sequences for *On the Town* than were seen in *Oklahoma!* The cast for *On the Town* included three couples in which the women were the more interesting characters and had more influence on the plot. The other crucial figure was director George Abbott, important in the development of musical comedy during the late 1930s in successful shows with Rodgers and Hart.[15] Abbott's entry into the project helped Smith and Feigay raise the necessary money, much of the total coming from MGM. Abbott

The Kansas City Ballet production of *Fancy Free*, October 2013. The three sailors fight over only two women.

served as the *éminence grise* for his younger collaborators, deleting portions of dialogue, songs and dances that he thought slowed the proceedings.[16]

Bernstein's score included more than ninety minutes of music, some of it sophisticated and dissonant by Broadway's standards, but, as in *Fancy Free*, there was effective use of jazz, blues and other vernacular styles. He wrote few hit songs for *On the Town*, but each number contributed to its dramatic situation. Bernstein relished his collaboration with Comden and Green. When 'Carried Away' was not working, they suggested that Bernstein try it in a minor key. That change, combined with their powerful voices (Comden and Green played Claire and Ozzie on stage), turned it into a highlight. That song and others such as 'Come Up to My Place' demonstrated Bernstein's gift for writing comic numbers, and the latter, sung by randy taxi driver Hildegard Esterhazy, included boogie-woogie and blues intervals. Hildegard, played by Nancy Walker, also sang 'I Can Cook, Too', a bluesy setting of a delightfully naughty text full of standard blues double meanings involving cooking and sexual innuendo. 'New York, New York' showed Bernstein's compositional sophistication, including blaring, dissonant chords in the opening fanfare and use of canon. More contemplative songs include 'Lonely Town', a lovely ballad, and 'Some Other Time', where the writers allowed the characters to conclude their 24 hours together poignantly, realizing that some aspects of their relationships would have to be explored later, stark reality for a nation at war.

Bernstein wrote his own dance music, a Broadway task usually taken by a dance arranger, and Robbins brought to the musical the same popular sensibility heard in *Fancy Free*. The character 'Ivy Smith' was played by Sono Osato, a member of the Ballet Theatre with previous Broadway experience.[17] Robbins used her classical training in 'Presentation of Miss Turnstiles', 'Lonely Town: Pas de Deux' and other dances. The choreography had its witty moments, but nobody would have mistaken some of the dancing in *On the*

Town for traditional Broadway hoofing. As in *Fancy Free*, Bernstein's dance music effectively combined classical and vernacular tropes, easily appreciated today by hearing 'Three Dance Episodes' from *On the Town*, Bernstein's concert suite for orchestra. Bernstein also worked on the show's orchestrations, sharing credit with four other arrangers.

On the Town opened on 28 December 1944 and was a hit, drawing rave reviews. In the *New York Times*, Lewis Nichols praised every aspect and recognized the show's careful integration: '"On the Town" is a perfect example of what a well-knit fusion of the respectable arts can provide for the theatre.'[18] Its run of 462 performances today seems short, but when it closed in early February 1946 the Second World War was over, ending the show's *raison d'être*. In its first Broadway revival in 1971 the show flopped, but subsequent revivals have been more successful, such as one that opened in 2014 and ran for 368 performances.[19] The original show broke new ground in several areas, especially racially: in addition to Sono Osato appearing in a lead role, there was a chorus of whites and African Americans appearing together and holding hands, and an African American pit conductor, Everett Lee. For Bernstein, *On the Town* was a personal, lucrative triumph, but during its Boston try-out he ran afoul of Koussevitzky, who enjoyed the show but then excoriated his protégé for wasting his talent on popular entertainment. Bernstein worked little on Broadway until after his mentor's death in 1951.

In addition to writing *On the Town*, in the last six months of 1944 Bernstein conducted *Fancy Free* on tour, guest conducted a number of orchestras and made political appearances. Bernstein lent his name to left-wing groups, a factor in the continuing growth of his FBI file.[20] He was interviewed often in the press and even appeared on radio game shows.

The New York City Symphony Orchestra

As 1945 started, Bernstein was one of the country's favourite guest conductors, booked by his manager Arthur Judson that year for fourteen different orchestras.[21] Bernstein also flirted with a Hollywood film project where he would have starred as Tchaikovsky and served as musical consultant, but it did not pan out. The one composition that Bernstein finished in 1945 was *Hashkiveinu*, a setting of a Jewish prayer for tenor, choir and organ commissioned by the Park Avenue Synagogue in New York, where it premiered on 11 May. It is an effective setting in ABA form with varied textures and vivid dynamic contrasts. The outer sections feature a chant-like melody developed over an extended pedal point in the organ, and the central section is faster with greater rhythmic interest.

In 1945 Bernstein landed his own orchestra: the New York City Symphony Orchestra. Recommended by Koussevitzky, Bernstein succeeded Leopold Stokowski. The ensemble formed in 1943 to play concerts at the City Center for Music and Dance in midtown Manhattan. According to newspaper accounts, Stokowski had been granted a leave of absence,[22] but Bernstein generated enough excitement to become indispensible. The appointment came from Mayor Fiorello LaGuardia, but the orchestra received no civic funds; receipts were meant to cover the ensemble's budget. As director Bernstein received no salary, just expenses, but he lived comfortably from royalties on his compositions.

Bernstein learned of his appointment on 25 August, his 27th birthday – the musician considered such coincidences providential. The season ran from October to April with twelve sets of moderately priced concerts on Mondays and Tuesdays. Bernstein auditioned a new orchestra and assembled a group of young musicians, retaining only one-third of the roster from the previous season, and put together an exciting slate of programmes.[23] The opening concert on 8 October included Copland's *An Outdoor Overture*, Shostakovich's Symphony no. 1 and Brahms's Symphony no. 2, which Olin Downes reviewed positively in the *New York Times*. He acknowledged that the ensemble's level of talent was not yet superb, but 'the performances were remindful of what a secondary matter technical finish is. All of the performances were stirring.' Downes concluded with rapt approval of Bernstein's new gig: 'We believe Mr. Bernstein is now in a good place, with an orchestra of young musicians like himself to work with, and a repertory to mature in. Here is a conductor.'[24]

Bernstein created a minor sensation over the next three seasons, causing a rivalry between his orchestra and the far better funded New York Philharmonic, still led by Rodzinski. Bernstein brought to his ensemble extraordinary energy and a flair for daring programming. He conducted nine of the twelve sets of concerts his first season, and all ten sets of performances in his other two seasons. Remarkably, every concert of the second and third seasons included a modern work in either its New York premiere or the work's second performance in the city, or another piece of distinctive interest.[25] For example, the programme first performed on 18 November 1946 included mostly unknown pieces by Alex North, John Lessard, Vladimir Dukelsky (Vernon Duke) and Samuel Barber, on a concert completed by Tchaikovsky's Symphony no. 6, 'Pathétique',[26] and a week later he offered six pieces by Stravinsky, including *Oedipus Rex* and the *Firebird Suite*. In addition to Copland's *An Outdoor Overture*, Bernstein also led the group in other concerts in his mentor's Piano Concerto and *Statements*, as well as Marc Blitzstein's *The Airborne Symphony*, a dramatic wartime work that Olin Downes called 'first class theatre' on its world premiere on 1 April 1946.[27]

Bernstein's last performance with the orchestra was a staged version of Blitzstein's *The Cradle Will Rock*. Some critics in the third season thought that standards had slipped a bit, including the *Herald Tribune*'s Virgil Thomson, who never liked Bernstein's energetic style of conducting and wrote a shrill review in which he questioned Bernstein's attachment to European culture and suggested that his career had become 'sheer vainglory'.[28] The orchestra was always a shoestring operation, Bernstein's third season made possible by a $10,000 donation by Local 802 of the American Federation of Musicians that was not to be renewed for another year.[29] Bernstein sought firmer financial footing and increases in the number of rehearsals, pay for musicians and the length of the season, and wanted there to be a salary for the director. The City Center chair Newbold Morris could not grant these requests, and Bernstein resigned. It was the last season for the New York City Symphony Orchestra, and Bernstein spent the next decade as a guest conductor.

Bernstein in Palestine

The existence of the Palestine Symphony Orchestra and its association with the Zionist movement was tailor-made for Bernstein's beliefs and ambitions. Polish violinist Bronisław Huberman founded the orchestra in 1936, seeing the ensemble 'as an embodiment of high cultural values that would represent the Jewish state before the world'.[30] Arturo Toscanini came to Palestine to direct the group's first concert, followed by other prominent guest conductors, such as William Steinberg and Sir Malcolm Sargent. The group had no permanent conductor.

Bernstein spoke on 28 May 1946 in New York before the American Fund for Palestinians, declaring his support for Zionism and that he could be of the most help to them by supporting their orchestra. He announced that he would be going to Palestine to conduct the group during spring 1947, an engagement that developed out of the orchestra contacting Bernstein in November 1945.[31] Subsequent communication from S. B. Lewertoff, an official with the orchestra, revealed that their manner of engaging conductors was to pay for their passage from Europe and their expenses while performing with the orchestra in Palestine and Egypt, but they could not afford to pay for their services. Bernstein agreed to lead the ensemble in conjunction with a European conducting tour in 1947.

His first tour in Israel included his father and sister. They sailed to Cherbourg and then went to Paris. One could only enter Palestine through Egypt, and Bernstein's outspoken Zionism made it challenging to obtain the necessary visa from the Egyptian embassy in Paris. There were also problems with boarding the plane from Cairo to Palestine. They arrived there in the midst of controversy and violence, but Bernstein's correspondence shows him revelling in the excitement and in his work with the orchestra. For example, he wrote to Koussevitzky: 'If you ever wanted to be involved in an historical moment, this is it. The people are remarkable; life goes on in spite of bombs, police, everything . . . The orchestra is fine, and I am having a great success.'[32]

Bernstein created his own explosion of excitement in Palestine. He performed nine concerts with the orchestra, which played at venues in several cities, none of which truly could be called concert halls. His programmes included works that Bernstein knew well: Robert Schumann's Symphony no. 2, Ravel's Piano Concerto in G with Bernstein as soloist/conductor, and his own Symphony no. 1, 'Jeremiah'. For his first three concerts he substituted Mozart's Symphony no. 36 for his own work, but the 'Jeremiah' was a resounding success once it was heard on 1 May in Jerusalem.[33] The symphony's delayed premiere in Palestine was caused by the score's disappearance in transit between Rome and Jerusalem. It had to be flown in from New York, giving Bernstein the thrill of the Jerusalem premiere.[34] Peter Gradenwitz, a prominent music critic in Palestine who became one of Bernstein's good friends and a future biographer, stated that the conductor 'is one of the most-talked of personalities and popular visiters [*sic*] in years.' Gradenwitz noted that 'not since the days of Arturo Toscanini – who, as you will remember, launched our orchestra on its way ten years ago – has a conductor been recalled so many times and been given a similar ovation.'[35] The orchestra's enthusiasm for Bernstein was assisted by the fact that he could work with them in Hebrew; the Palestine Symphony offered Bernstein its directorship later that summer. He turned it down but stated that he hoped to remain an important figure with the orchestra, the beginnings of a complicated dance between him and the ensemble that lasted for the rest of his life.

Bernstein conducting a rehearsal at Carnegie Hall, *c.* 1946–8.

Before returning to the United States, Bernstein pursued the remainder of his tour, the highlights of which included leading the European premiere of Copland's Symphony no. 3 (about which Bernstein wrote the composer a cheeky letter[36]) in Prague and concerts in Paris, Brussels and The Hague. On his return to New York, he conducted the New York Philharmonic in four concerts at Lewisohn Stadium and then went to Tanglewood for the summer season, becoming the first conductor besides Koussevitzky to lead the Boston Symphony Orchestra in festival concerts.

Disappointment and Indecision

Bernstein's burgeoning career did not preclude other possibilities in the States and developments in his personal life. Koussevitzky had continued his generous sponsorship of Bernstein, providing fabulous opportunities, like leading the American premiere of Benjamin Britten's opera *Peter Grimes* at Tanglewood in summer 1946 and placing his protégé on the podium before the Boston Symphony Orchestra in performances in Boston, New York's Carnegie Hall, Tanglewood and a broadcast concert. The Boston maestro hoped that Bernstein would succeed him as music director, but in retrospect it would have been highly unlikely that the conservative organization would have handed their directorship to a hometown, Jewish boy less than thirty years old who had written a Broadway musical, was heard playing boogie-woogie and cultivated the popular press. His rumoured homosexuality also surely weighed against such an appointment. The Boston Symphony Orchestra named Charles Munch as Koussevitzky's successor in April 1948.

The most significant development in Bernstein's personal life had been meeting Felicia Montealegre Cohn in February 1946, the woman he would marry in 1951. She was an actress who worked on stage and in television. Born in Chile, daughter of a wealthy, Jewish American mining engineer and a Chilean mother, she had come to New York to study the piano, but she became more interested in acting. There is considerable evidence that Bernstein kept seeing other men and women after meeting Felicia, but by the autumn of 1946 they were dating regularly.[37] In December Bernstein travelled to Hollywood to investigate a film opportunity (which ultimately yielded nothing), and Felicia went with him to look into acting opportunities. Bernstein's letters to Helen Coates report that they were drifting towards becoming engaged while Koussevitzky urged Bernstein to marry Felicia without delay,[38] thereby silencing doubts about Bernstein's sexuality. They announced their engagement before the end of 1946, but Bernstein was ambivalent about marriage, and their first engagement ended in late 1947.[39] When they finally did marry in 1951, it was with Bernstein's greater interest in her and after Koussevitzky's death, a major watershed moment for the young musician.

Compositions Major and Minor

A frenetic travel schedule as a guest conductor/pianist slowed Bernstein's compositional activities, but did not end them. His lifelong battle between performing and finding a quiet place where he might conceive his own music was one of Bernstein's greatest challenges. Those who find his music compelling probably should be grateful that he wrote as much as he did.

His first major effort between the end of the Second World War and his marriage in 1951 was the ballet *Facsimile* (1946), another collaboration with Jerome Robbins. While conceiving the work, their imaginations easily drifted to psychology; both men were involved in analysis. Just after Bernstein directed the American premiere of *Peter Grimes* in August 1946, Robbins came to Tanglewood and they developed a scenario involving three lonely people – two men and a woman – who desire personal connections but only manage 'facsimiles' of relationships. Bernstein composed the nineteen-minute score in August and made a piano recording for the dancers to begin work. The Ballet Theatre premiered *Facsimile* unsuccessfully on 24 October. Perhaps the major problem was that it was not like the charming and funny *Fancy Free*. John Martin, dance critic for the *New York Times*, offered grudging admiration: 'Not an ingratiating piece, by any means, it nevertheless commands respect and raises its creator [Robbins] several notches in the scale of artistic accomplishment.' Martin called the music 'eminently theatrical, making brilliant use of instrumental colour contrasts, getting as turbid sometimes in its syncopations as Mr. Robbins' complicated lifts, but containing some beautifully musical passages for all that'.[40] Neither dance nor music entered the permanent repertory.

For concerts, Bernstein prepared *Facsimile: A Choreographic Essay*, which caused a disagreement with Koussevitzky when Bernstein tried to perform it in a series of concerts that he was leading with the Boston Symphony Orchestra. His mentor wrote him a scathing letter on 23 December, leaving little doubt of what he thought of Bernstein's compositions: 'May I ask you: do you think that your composition is worthy of the Boston Symphony Orchestra and the Boston organization? Can it be placed on the same level as Beethoven, Schubert, Brahms, Stravinsky, Prokofieff, Bartók, or Copland?' He also asserted that only the orchestra's 'permanent conductor' should programme 'works of lesser value'.[41] Although perhaps not a work that will ever be famous, *Facsimile* again demonstrated that Bernstein could write effective music on which to base movement. Composed in four major sections, it is a disciplined development of the opening material for oboe and flute with several sections that demonstrate Bernstein's characteristic lyricism and rhythmic interest. As in *Fancy Free*, he uses piano as a solo instrument, but less often in jazz or blues style here. Copland appears to have been a major inspiration for *Facsimile*.

The period included several sets of short pieces for various performing forces. For voice he composed the song cycle *La Bonne cuisine* (1947), and *Two Love Songs* (1949) on texts by Rainer Maria Rilke. The former, four settings of Bernstein's translations of old French recipes, demonstrates Bernstein's comfort with light texts. The cycle is very short and the songs range from moderately fast to *presto*. Bernstein dedicated both *La Bonne cuisine* and *Two Love Songs* to mezzo-soprano Jennie Tourel, who premiered the Rilke pieces separately in 1949 and 1963. The first, 'Extinguish My Eyes', springs forward breathlessly, as a desperate lover parts from the paramour. 'When My Soul Touches Yours' is slower and reflective, but with an active accompaniment.

Four Anniversaries (1948) and *Five Anniversaries* (1949–51) were the second and third collections of piano miniatures that Bernstein published, each a tribute to a friend or colleague. The 1948 set included movements dedicated to Felicia Montealegre; Johnny Mehegan, a jazz pianist that Bernstein fell in love with at Tanglewood in 1947;[42] David Diamond, a friend and fellow composer; and Helen Coates, his secretary. The next set, except for a tribute to composer/conductor Lukas Foss, includes dedications to children of friends. *Brass Music* (1948) is five movements for various solo brass instruments (trumpet, horn, trombone, tuba), and a finale for brass quartet. Each is named after a friend's pet. They are varied and witty pieces, some of which get played often.

Jazz clarinettist Woody Herman asked Bernstein to write a piece in 1949 for his Second Herd, but the ensemble had disbanded before the completion of *Prelude, Fugue and Riffs*. Bernstein tried to use it as a ballet in *Wonderful Town* (1953), but the segment was cut. He premiered the piece on an *Omnibus* broadcast, 'The World of Jazz', on 16 October 1955. Although based on jazz idioms, the work includes only limited improvisation in *ad libitum* repetitions towards the conclusion. The 'Prelude' is a jaunty, bluesy movement for trumpets and trombones, while the delightful 'Fugue' is for five saxophones. 'Riffs' is a clarinet solo accompanied by band and includes the piece's most characteristic jazz sound. Bernstein dedicated the piece to jazz clarinettist Benny Goodman, with whom he recorded it.

The one work that Bernstein wrote in this period that became a major part of his lasting compositional legacy was Symphony no. 2, 'The Age of Anxiety' (1949). Despite what Koussevitzky had thought of *Facsimile*, his foundation commissioned this symphony. Bernstein turned for inspiration to British poet W. H. Auden's *The Age of Anxiety: A Baroque Eclogue* (1947), a lengthy poem exploring contemporary Western culture. Despite mixed reviews, it won the Pulitzer Prize for Poetry in 1948. The idea of using the poem as grist for a composition appears to have come from Richard Adams 'Twig' Romney, a friend who wrote to Bernstein on 25 July 1947 mentioning Auden's work as a possible source for 'a tone poem'.[43] In a letter four days later, after having heard from Bernstein that perhaps it might make a good ballet, Romney urged the composer to keep the work 'in the concert hall' where he could 'protect it from being too obvious program music', allowing that later it might perhaps become a ballet.[44] Romney's prescience was notable: Jerome Robbins fitted choreography to Bernstein's piece in 1950.

Bernstein's second symphony illustrates the conundrum of genre identification that exists in several of his works. 'The Age of Anxiety' has a large solo piano part, causing the piece to sound much like a concerto, but piano concertos seldom carry programmes. Bernstein, therefore, called the piece a symphony. His frequent combination of elements from multiple genres sometimes confused reviewers and audiences.

Auden's poem includes four characters – Quant, Malin, Emble and Rosetta – who meet in a New York City bar. The author's thoughts emerge in their dialogue at a bar, in a cab and at Rosetta's apartment. Some critics have tried to minimize the relationship between symphony and poem, including biographer Humphrey Burton, who raises doubts because Bernstein used music written for earlier projects in the work.[45] Allen Shawn seems closer to the truth when he demonstrates how faithfully Bernstein followed Auden's structure with his symphony. Both works are divided into two large sections, each with three sub-sections: 'Prologue – Seven Ages – Seven Stages'; 'Dirge – Masque – Epilogue'.[46] Instrumental music does not allow Bernstein to describe explicitly his reaction to Auden's poem, or its dramatic progress, but the composer appears to have intended to honour the literary work in the spirit of less specific, nineteenth-century programme music.

'Prologue' is a lonely clarinet duet, music that Bernstein had used in the past, in *The Birds* in 1941 and as a birthday greeting for Koussevitzky in 1944. The short segment concludes with a descending scale in the flute, introducing an introspective passage for piano based on similar material that opens the fourteen variations that Bernstein wrote to represent the 'Seven Ages' and 'Seven Stages'. Each variation builds on material heard earlier, and although each section is distinctive, one has the feeling of continuous development, analogous to the conversations in Auden's poem. Interplay between piano and orchestra, and among various sections within the larger ensemble, is memorable and demonstrates Bernstein's fine grasp of orchestration. A new, impassioned melody in the strings, reminiscent of Bartók, opens 'Seven Stages', widening the thematic palette, but previous material continues to be grist for the variation mill. Towards the end of the symphony's first half, piano and orchestra rush to a powerful climax.

In the 'Dirge', Bernstein plays with all twelve chromatic pitches, revelling in potential dissonances through material that Shawn describes as 'ritualistic', reaching a thunderous climax that precedes the return of earlier material.[47] The 'Masque' begins with a jazz-like theme in the piano that sounds like late swing or bop, not unlike the way the piano plays the role of jazz commentator in *Fancy Free*. The section includes the theme from 'Ain't Got No Tears Left', a song cut from *On the Town*, and the affect of 'Masque' evokes the party atmosphere enjoyed by Auden's quartet of philosophical imbibers.

Bernstein's 'Epilogue' perhaps demonstrates what first drew him to the poem. Rosetta is Jewish, and before Auden's 'Epilogue' she references the Holocaust and invokes the *Sh'ma Yisra'el*, the Jewish declaration that 'Hear O Israel, The Lord our God, the Lord is One!'[48] For Bernstein, this was probably a moving moment in the poem. In the 'Epilogue' he brings back a motive (A-flat down to E-flat and D-flat, returning to the same A-flat) from his previous symphony, 'Jeremiah', which Jack Gottlieb discovered in a number of Bernstein's works and believes represents the declaration 'Jehovah'.[49] The original version of the symphony ended with little heard from the piano, but Bernstein substantially revised the conclusion in 1965, augmenting the piano's participation. Bernstein premiered the symphony on 8 April 1949, playing the piano solo with Koussevitzky conducting the Boston Symphony Orchestra. Reviews were mixed, but Symphony no. 2, 'The Age of Anxiety', remains one of Bernstein's more convincing major works.

Despite Koussevitzky's wish that he avoid work in the popular theatre, Bernstein accepted a commission to write incidental music for a production of J. M. Barrie's play *Peter Pan*, composed while on holiday in Florida in December 1949.[50] By his own admission, the composer got carried away and wrote the requested dances and segments to set moods, plus five songs and two choruses, for which he also wrote the lyrics.[51] The music bears a simplicity and sweetness unusual for Bernstein, evoking a child's world. Simplicity and directness of expression are common in Copland's music, such as the spare diatonicism of his film score for *Our Town*. Although this may not have been a direct influence on Bernstein, he certainly knew this aspect of Copland's music. Bernstein was in Europe when *Peter Pan* opened on 24 April 1950; his friend Marc Blitzstein revised the score as necessary during rehearsals, a process that was more difficult than Bernstein had expected, as Blitzstein outlined in a letter from 16 April.[52] Bernstein's music from *Peter Pan* was barely known for decades, but it has now been recorded.[53]

A Whirlwind of Guest Conducting

The first American-born, American-trained orchestral conductor to have an international career, Bernstein became proficient at working with ensembles that he did not know, choosing repertory to which he brought understanding and excitement. He continued to perform piano concertos with orchestras while conducting. Critical responses to his work varied, of course – some reviewers never warmed to his athletic, emotive conducting style – but Bernstein was often asked to return to ensembles and had all the work he could handle. Although he often wrote in letters to friends or said in interviews that he wanted to suspend his conducting career so that he could compose more, he seldom managed to do this. Here his guest conducting will be approached through mention of major tours and concerts of special importance.

After the fabulous success of his first trip to Palestine, Bernstein was scheduled to return in February 1948, before another European conducting season. He cancelled that trip for health reasons. He was able to keep the cause of his condition secret, but Burton has speculated that he suffered from his first bout of emphysema.[54] Whatever the reason, Bernstein uncharacteristically relaxed for much of the first two months of 1948. In March he discussed the position of artistic director with an official from the Palestine Symphony Orchestra who had come to the United States; Bernstein accepted the position in the spring after he learned that he would not succeed Koussevitzky at the Boston Symphony Orchestra.[55] Later in the year the Palestine Symphony Orchestra insisted that the title be changed to 'musical adviser', perhaps because Bernstein would not agree to stay for the entire season.[56] What he did for the orchestra in the autumn of 1948, however, in the early months after Israel had declared itself a nation and while its War of Independence raged, could only be called extraordinary.

After successful concerts in Munich (unusual for a Jewish-American conductor so soon after the war), an emotional concert with Jewish survivors of the concentration camp at Dachau, work in Milan, Budapest, Vienna and Paris, and another season at Tanglewood in July and August, Bernstein arrived in Israel on 25 September 1948 and stayed for more than two months. With concerts presented in multiple cities and more than once in most locations, he conducted 38 performances and served as piano soloist in 32 of them.[57] Several performances occurred close to the front lines, such as one at Rehovoth on 21 October that was interrupted twice by air raid sirens.[58] His programming mixed traditional and modern, ranging from Mozart and Beethoven to Schumann, Brahms, Mahler, Gershwin, Ravel, Bartók, Copland, his own *Fancy Free* and other composers. One of the most memorable moments of Bernstein's career took place at Beersheba on 20 November, where he travelled in a bus with 35 volunteers from the orchestra for a concert in support of soldiers holding the area in defiance of a United Nations order. They played outdoors at an archaeological dig with Bernstein leading the entire performance from the piano: Beethoven's Concerto no. 1, Mozart's Concerto no. 15 and Gershwin's *Rhapsody in Blue*. Such bravado made Bernstein a national hero.[59] The last programme of the visit, performed six times in Tel Aviv, Jerusalem and Haifa in late November, included Bach's Brandenburg Concerto no. 3 and Mahler's Symphony no. 2, 'Resurrection', the latter boldly associated by Bernstein with the 'rebirth' of Israel.[60] It was an enormous work and less famous than it is today, challenging the orchestra by the logistics of providing a large chorus, and challenging in a country that looked askance at Mahler's conversion to Catholicism, but all six concerts sold out. The ensemble, now called the Israel Philharmonic, again offered Bernstein its directorship under generous terms, but he gave no firm answer and left for his conducting debut in Rome.[61] Bernstein finally refused the post by telegram on 31 December 1948, but said that he would return to Israel in 1950. The orchestra named French conductor Paul Paray as artistic director for the 1949–50 season without consulting Bernstein. He was outraged by the choice, but also unwilling to commit himself.[62]

In spring 1949 MGM Studios was ready to make a film of *On the Town*, to be directed by Stanley Donen and Gene Kelly, who also starred with Frank Sinatra, Ann Miller and others. The studio did not want to use all of Bernstein's music because of a lack of hit tunes and the fact that Bernstein's ownership of the rights limited their profitability. They paid him a consulting fee of $5,000 that allowed them to change the score, and most of his songs were removed in favour of new ones by composer Roger Edens with lyrics by Comden and Green.[63] Bernstein worked on the second act ballet with Gene Kelly. It was a successful film, but only marginally part of Bernstein's legacy.

In summer 1949 Bernstein did three concerts with the Philadelphia Orchestra at their summer home at Robin Hood Dell. In one of those performances he first performed Wagner's *Tristan and Isolde* in a concert version with noted Wagnerian singers Lauritz Melchior and Helen Traubel. Although Wagner's well-known anti-Semitism gave Bernstein pause, he loved the music drama and later performed and recorded it. In July and August Bernstein was again Koussevitzky's assistant at Tanglewood, where they reprised 'The Age of Anxiety' with the composer as soloist.

The 1949–50 concert season included appearances with a number of important American orchestras and leading the New York Philharmonic in 'The Age of Anxiety' with Lukas Foss at the piano in February, the same week when Jerome Robbins's ballet based on the symphony premiered in New York. A project that demonstrated Bernstein's exceptional ability to deal with challenging scores occurred in November when he led the world premiere with the Boston Symphony Orchestra of Olivier Messiaen's *Turangalila Symphony*. Since this work is ten movements in length and fiendishly difficult, taking it as a world premiere required the ability to teach it to the orchestra in addition to interpreting it without previous models. After leading the premiere in Boston, Bernstein and the orchestra took the piece to Carnegie Hall, where Olin Downes applauded the conductor's work: 'Mr. Bernstein did a perfectly amazing job with an extremely difficult score, deserving any and all recognition that could be given him for his accomplishment.'[64] Another important development was Bernstein signing his first recording contract with Columbia Records in January 1950, the company with which he worked for the next two decades.

The spring found Bernstein in Italy for three weeks followed by his next jaunt to Israel for May and June, where he performed 'The Age of Anxiety' ten times while conducting from the keyboard, an act of considerable bravado. He had done it in Turin, Italy, when a conductor proved inadequate and decided to perform the work that way also in Israel, as he reported in a letter to his sister Shirley on 26 April 1950.[65] His schedule in Israel included five separate concerts, most played several times; collaborating soloists included violinist Jascha Heifetz and pianist Alexis Weissenberg. Bernstein's programming was wide-ranging and notable for its numerous American works, including one concert of Roy Harris's Symphony no. 3, Carlos Chávez's *Sinfonía india*, Copland's 'Four Dance Episodes' from *Rodeo* and Gershwin's *Rhapsody in Blue* with Bernstein conducting from the keyboard.[66]

His most ambitious programme was the last, including Mahler's *Das Lied von der Erde*.

This whirlwind of activity continued for Bernstein through the summer of 1950. Travelling with siblings Shirley and Burton, he conducted in the Netherlands in the first two weeks of July and was at the Edinburgh Festival in late August with the Orchestre National de la RTF, followed by more conducting in the Netherlands. On 30 August Bernstein for the first time led Beethoven's Symphony no. 9, with the Residentie Orchestra of The Hague, which he described in a letter to his parents as 'a triumph!'[67] In November he worked for the first time with the orchestra at La Scala in concerts that included Mahler's Symphony no. 2 and Stravinsky's *The Rite of Spring*.

His work with the Israel Philharmonic continued soon thereafter. He returned in December 1950 for two concerts before accompanying the orchestra to the United States, where they toured from coast to coast for three months with Bernstein and Koussevitzky. Bernstein substituted at times for his mentor, who was not well; in three months he led the ensemble in 28 concerts, leaving the tour to perform with other orchestras, such as the New York Philharmonic in February for the world premiere of the difficult Symphony no. 2 by Charles Ives, composed almost fifty years before.

Once the Israeli tour ended, Bernstein went to Mexico City to work for a week with Carlos Chávez's National Symphony Orchestra, ending a memorable year in which he had conducted about a hundred concerts with twelve different orchestras.[68] He went on to Cuernavaca, where he found a house near his friend Martha Gellhorn, a writer who had once been married to Ernest Hemingway. Bernstein stayed for several weeks, relaxing and working on his opera *Trouble in Tahiti*.

A Change of Life

Bernstein had stopped in Phoenix at Koussevitzky's winter home
after conducting the last three concerts of the Israel Philharmonic
tour in New York in spring 1951. He did not find the elderly maestro
well. He rushed to Boston from Mexico at the beginning of June
when Koussevitzky's wife Olga phoned to tell him that the aged
Russian conductor was worse, and Bernstein arrived in time to
spend hours with his mentor the night of 3 June, the day before he
died. Bernstein attended the funeral services and graveside service
in Lenox, near Koussevitzky's beloved Tanglewood.

Koussevitzky's demise corresponded with the re-entry of Felicia
Montealegre Cohn into Bernstein's life. She had moved on since her
engagement to Bernstein ended in late 1947, becoming one of the
up-and-coming young female stars in television drama and working
on the New York stage. She was living with the actor Dick Hart, who
was married with children and drank heavily. Bernstein, as seen in
letters that he wrote to his sister Shirley, had been having serious
second thoughts about Felicia; he asked Shirley, still friends with
Felicia, to speak to her in spring 1950.[69] When Hart died of a heart
attack in January 1951, Shirley urged her brother to console Felicia.
It was a complicated, unpredictable road, including Bernstein
going to Mexico alone for weeks and Felicia taking a solo trip to
Europe while writing affectionate letters to Bernstein, but in the end
she rediscovered her love for him and he decided to try marriage
and children, a strong impulse for the Jewish Bernstein.[70] It was
at Tanglewood, where Bernstein had taken over the conducting
department following Koussevitzky's death, that Felicia finally
forced him to make a commitment. Felicia converted to Judaism
(she was raised Roman Catholic, but her father was Jewish), and
they married at Temple Mishkan Tefila on 9 September 1951. The
newlyweds embarked on a five-week drive that went all the way to
San Francisco and then on to Cuernavaca.

As Simeone has noted, Bernstein apparently considered his marriage a trial arrangement.[71] He wrote to his brother Burton on 18 September that he and Felicia had had a 'big crisis' while staying with his friends Philip and Barbara Marcuse in Detroit, but the Marcuses helped mediate.[72] Three weeks later, Bernstein wrote to the Marcuses, noting that tensions still existed, but there were also moments of calm for the couple. He declared that they would have to see how things developed in 'a marriage contracted in insecurity'.[73] In a strange juxtaposition, Bernstein's compositional project continued to be his opera *Trouble in Tahiti*, which concerns a troubled marriage. While in Cuernavaca, Bernstein's friend Martha Gellhorn spent much time with them and came to feel a bit like their nanny.[74] The couple remained in Mexico until February 1952, when Felicia received an acting offer that she did not wish to refuse, and Bernstein had been asked to fill in for an ailing Charles Munch at the Boston Symphony Orchestra in February and March.

The way forward for them seems to be suggested by a letter that Felicia wrote to her husband sometime early in their marriage. He had just left for a week, and the letter shows her progressive thinking about homosexuality.[75] She admits that their marriage might not last and that 'you are a homosexual and may never change – you don't admit to the possibility of a double life, but if your piece of mind, your health, your whole nervous system depend on a certain sexual pattern what can you do?' She avows her love for him and willingness to accept him as he is 'without being a martyr' and states, 'let's try and see what happens if you are free to do as you like, but without guilt and confession, please!' She wants to try to stay married, perhaps 'not based on passion but on tenderness and mutual respect'. Bernstein had permission to pursue relationships with men, and Felicia wished to remain ignorant of them. What might have solidified their relationship was their offspring. She was carrying Jamie when they left Mexico in December 1951; the birth was near their first anniversary. Alexander followed in 1955, Nina in 1962. Bernstein was crazy about them, and in future years wrote Felicia many letters stating his love for her. The marriage might not have been easy, but Felicia was, except perhaps for music, the one consuming and lengthy love of Leonard Bernstein's life.

4

'I simply must decide what I'm going to be when I grow up': Leaning Towards Composition, 1952–7

The period between Bernstein's marriage and his appointment as music director of the New York Philharmonic included his most intensive work as a composer, including completion of three Broadway scores, an opera and a violin concerto.[1] Despite all of this creative activity, however, Bernstein still found time for guest conducting, the start of his television career and teaching at Brandeis University, on top of his home life in New York City with Felicia and their first two children. To be sure, some of the conducting and television work was partly for the money – Bernstein's lifestyle with Felicia was expensive – but it is also clear that it was not easy for him to simply stop other activities and compose. Broadway work is collaborative, and probably was more engrossing to this active extrovert than creating by himself, and in his theatrical works in this period one finds some of the best music that he ever wrote. As Allen Shawn has noted, this was the period when Bernstein's compositional ideas flowed most easily.[2]

Two Festivals and *Trouble in Tahiti*

Bernstein's mentor Koussevitzky had advised Brandeis University in Waltham, Massachusetts, on musical matters during its formation, so it was perhaps his mentor's association with the school that encouraged Bernstein to accept a visiting professorship there in

1952. It was not the most convenient position for a globetrotting guest conductor who also composed, but Bernstein threw himself into projects there when in residence. His first commitment was the directorship of an ambitious Festival of the Creative Arts in June 1952. Bernstein had committed to completing his opera *Trouble in Tahiti* to be premiered at the festival, in addition to a busy schedule performing and serving on various panels.

Upon returning from Mexico in February, Bernstein went to Boston to conduct for three weeks and then settled in at Yaddo, an artist's colony outside Saratoga, New York, where in five weeks he finished composing and orchestrating *Trouble in Tahiti*. The festival at Brandeis lasted from 12–15 June.[3] The first night included a lengthy symposium on the state of the arts in the United States, followed by the opera's premiere, which did not start until around 11 p.m., outdoors before an audience of about three thousand. The next afternoon included discussion of Dixieland jazz and bop featuring such performers as Miles Davis, Lee Konitz and Max Roach. Other activities included the premiere of Blitzstein's new translation of *The Threepenny Opera*, with the translator narrating, Bernstein conducting, and Weill's widow Lotte Lenya in her original role of Jenny, which she also played in G.W. Pabst's German-language film version; dancer Merce Cunningham performing to a piece of *musique concrète* by Pierre Schaeffer and Pierre Henry and choreographing Stravinsky's *Les Noces*; and Bernstein conducting the Boston Symphony Orchestra strings and a few other instruments in a programme of music by William Schuman, Irving Fine, Ben Weber, Benjamin Britten and Aaron Copland. This was in addition to poetry readings, symposia, exhibitions and documentary screenings. It was a strenuous four days, but audiences for main events numbered in the thousands. Bernstein helped Brandeis quickly develop a national profile. The second Festival of the Creative Arts, called 'The Comic Spirit', took place in June 1953 with the participation of cartoonists Al Capp and

Saul Steinberg and writer S. J. Perelman.[4] The music budget was smaller, with one programme that Bernstein conducted featuring Morton Gould's Concerto for Tap-dancer and Orchestra with soloist Danny Daniels and Francis Poulenc's opera *Les Mamelles de Tirésias*. This was the last Brandeis festival in which Bernstein was involved; the springtime event honours his memory today as the Leonard Bernstein Festival of the Creative Arts. Bernstein's relationship with Brandeis continued for a few more years and included memorable classes, especially a seminar in 1954 in which Bernstein shared compositional problems that he was wrestling with in *Candide* and had students work out their own solutions. He brought in collaborators, such as book writer Lillian Hellman, to help him evaluate student compositions. Many composers are guarded about unfinished works; this seems to have been an act of extraordinary generosity on Bernstein's part. One of the students was Jack Gottlieb, who later became his assistant and was associated with Bernstein's office for years.[5]

The reception of *Trouble in Tahiti* at the first Brandeis festival was disappointing. Bernstein began revisions quickly, writing to David Diamond on 21 July 1952:

> My little opera was a dud at Brandeis, due mostly to the half-baked state in which it found itself at première time; but now the revisions are almost finished, and a new (the true) ending composed; and I look forward to a more reasonable and telling production here at T'wood on 10 August.[6]

While in charge of the conducting school at Tanglewood that summer, Bernstein managed two performances of the opera's revised version with stage director Sarah Caldwell. Burton reports that audiences appreciated the work, but some reviewers remained dismissive.[7] Writing in the *New York Times*, Olin Downes found the work unrealistic: 'This is emotionally dilettantish, unreal. It can

Bernstein conducting *The Threepenny Opera* at Brandeis University Festival of Creative Arts with Kurt Weill's widow Lotte Lenya singing in the middle of the stage with her arm extended, 1952.

hardly produce interesting music.'[8] Bernstein, however, did not give up on the piece, conducting it in a live television broadcast on 16 November 1952, and allowing it to be part of a triple bill on Broadway called *All in One* that opened on 19 April 1955 and ran for 47 performances. The 45-minute opera remains in the repertory, especially at the college level; its brevity compromises professional possibilities. Bernstein returned to the same characters in the revised version of his later opera *A Quiet Place*.

Trouble in Tahiti reveals much about Bernstein; it is one of his few musical theatre works with no collaborators – Bernstein also wrote the libretto. He drew on the experience of the unhappy marriage between his parents but updated the subject, writing about a discontented couple living in a 'perfect' suburb of post-war America. The man is Sam, his father's name, and the woman is Dinah, named for Bernstein's paternal grandmother. As in the ballet *Facsimile*, these people struggle to make a real connection, arguing incessantly and avoiding contact. Sam is cocksure of himself and his prowess in business and handball. Dinah lacks confidence and is desperately sad. Neither manages to attend their son's school play, with Sam at a handball tournament and Dinah seeking escape by attending the film *Trouble in Tahiti*. When Sam comes home he cannot bring himself to have a productive conversation with Dinah, suggesting instead that they attend the same film she saw that afternoon. She agrees. Bernstein provided a moment of comic relief with Dinah's solo reaction to the film, the aria 'What a movie!', lampooning celluloid escapism. Jazzy trios poke fun at Madison Avenue conventions and the wonderful life one was supposed to find in the suburbs, but *Trouble in Tahiti* is a bleak look at American life and marriage in the early 1950s.

Bernstein admirably played the role of social commentator here. The trio sings a devastating imitation of slick commercial jingles, and the composer brings a clear sense of American speech rhythms to such segments as the opening argument between Sam and Dinah (Scene 1) and Sam's phone conversations at the office (Scene 2), the latter punctuated by the trio assuring Sam of his talents. Bernstein's refined sense of lyricism dominates Scene 3, with Dinah in her analyst's office, and when Sam and Dinah run into each other and avoid lunching together in Scene 4, especially in their joint soliloquies. Sam's bluster after his victory at the gym (Scene 5) is pointedly ironic, and other segments also confirm that Bernstein could secure effective characterization as librettist and composer. Themes recur intelligently, such as motives from Scene 1 returning in Scene 7 when the couple comes back together, and Bernstein reveals throughout his gift for writing for voices. Those who find the plot difficult must consider that operas often explore uncomfortable behaviour. Bernstein believed in the power of musical theatre to comment upon foibles and conflicts, which he also did not avoid in musicals that he wrote in the 1950s.

Wonderful Town

Bernstein's frenetic life in 1952 included the birth of his eldest child with Felicia, their daughter Jamie, on 8 September 1952. Fatherhood appears to have fulfilled a lifelong dream for Bernstein and it was a role that he relished. Felicia continued with her acting career to an extent and at times travelled with her husband. Burton often reports cash flow problems for the couple during the 1950s,[9] but those diminished as time passed and Bernstein became conductor of the New York Philharmonic, recorded more for Columbia and began to reap ample royalties from *West Side Story*.

With Koussevitzky gone, Bernstein was apparently more open to scoring a Broadway musical, and an opportunity came in the autumn of 1952. George Abbott and Robert Fryer had negotiated bringing film star Rosalind Russell to New York to recreate her role of Ruth Sherwood from the film *My Sister Eileen* (1942), based upon Ruth McKenney's stories. Joseph Fields and Jerome Chodorov, who had written the 1940 play by the same name and the Hollywood screenplay, wrote the book for the musical, but Abbott's first choices to write the score had not produced anything useful, and they needed to get into production before losing their option on Russell. Abbott returned to his collaborators from *On the Town*, convincing Betty Comden and Adolph Green to write lyrics, and then Bernstein agreed to compose the music. They had to hurry, and composed the score between early November and mid-December.

Fields and Chodorov wanted to update the story from the 1930s, but Bernstein's initial inspiration was his love for swing jazz. He especially remembered a vamp popularized by 1930s bandleader Eddy Duchin, a memory that he worked into the score with the designation 'Molto "Duchino"' for the opening song, 'Christopher Street'.[10] The exuberance of Bernstein, Comden and Green won out and the story remained in the 1930s, one of several battles with Fields and Chodorov. Abbott approved of what his songwriting team wanted to do with the show, making it more satirical, but remembered the arguments: 'There was more hysterical debate, more acrimony, more tension and more screaming connected with this play than with any other show I was ever involved with.'[11] Despite the decibel level, Abbott brought his usual level of professionalism to the production and the show was in fine shape during its out-of-town tryouts in Boston and Philadelphia. The choreographer was Donald Saddler, but Jerome Robbins (working uncredited) came in to polish the dances. *Wonderful Town* premiered on 25 February 1953 and embarked on a fine Broadway run of 559 performances, winning eight Tony Awards, including Best Musical.

The plot involves two sisters from Columbus, Ohio, Ruth and Eileen Sherwood, who move to New York's Greenwich Village. Ruth has designs on a writing career and Eileen wants to make it in show business. They find little success but meet interesting people, including Baker, an editor, who falls in love with Ruth. Eileen is the prettier of the two, but she does not find real love. The tendency of men to fawn over her, such as an entire police station in the mock-Irish number 'My Darling Eileen', is humorous, but, as Eileen confesses in song, she only falls 'A Little Bit in Love', a ballad that beautifully captures her contrasting virginal and come-hither qualities. Edith Adams was effective as Eileen, but *Wonderful Town* was created for Rosalind Russell, and she was brilliant, combining deft comic timing, devil-may-care physicality and an unforgettably low voice. Bernstein, Comden and Green accommodated her poor singing ability with such numbers as 'One Hundred Easy Ways', which Russell largely spoke her way through. In the midst of raving about the show, Brooks Atkinson stated in the *New York Times* about Russell that 'she makes the whole city wonderful . . .'.[12] Once Russell left the show, Carol Channing replaced her, but some of the magic disappeared. *Wonderful Town* closed and went on tour with Channing remaining in the role of Ruth.

Like that of *On the Town*, the score to *Wonderful Town* is a satisfying combination of comic gestures, varied types of songs, references to vernacular styles, specific musical characterization and genuine lyricism. The opening, 'Christopher Street', is an ingenious combination of commercial gestures that introduce Greenwich Village and the show's madcap sensibility. 'Ohio' is mockingly serious with ideal lyrics, somewhat like a melody for a country song. 'One Hundred Easy Ways' includes commercial blues tropes, while 'What a Waste' is classically conceived at its opening, smacking of Blitzstein and Copland, but becomes an energetic Broadway song. The introduction includes a reference to 'Ohio', an example of Bernstein tying together the score's songs. 'Pass the Football', a tribute to stupid jocks with outrageous rhymes, plays with swing and blues. 'Conversation Piece' is a wonderfully crafted musical scene that captures an awkward party where nobody knows what to say, exploded by Bernstein's chaotic ending dominated by Edie Adams's coloratura. 'A Quiet Girl' is a sweet ballad – unusual for Bernstein – but it carries a sense of irony because Baker sings about Ruth, who hardly exemplifies the title. 'Conga!' is a wild dance number brought on by Ruth interviewing Brazilian cadets who just want to learn the dance. Bernstein's music is characteristic and the lyrics feature some of Comden's and Green's cleverest list rhymes. Bernstein's regard for music of the 1930s is displayed with aplomb in 'Swing!', where Ruth demonstrates her inability to feel the music while carrying a sign for the Village Vortex, but the song becomes a production number for passing hipsters. 'It's Love' is a conventional ballad for Baker that relates motivically to 'A Little Bit in Love'. The earlier song includes several phrases that open with Eileen humming a descending perfect fifth, but most of the phrases that Baker sings start with an ascending fifth. Eileen convinces him that he is in love with Ruth. 'Ballet at the Village Vortex' is precisely the 'Slow heavy blues' that Bernstein designates at the head of the score,[13] introducing the final scene at the club where

Eileen and Ruth sing 'The Wrong Note Rag', an uproarious number that includes numerous repetitions of short motives and frequent, irritating half-steps.

In ironic counterpoint to the successful musical comedy, the McCarthy Era affected Bernstein and his friends before and during the show's run. Both Copland and Bernstein were named as Communists along with many other noted figures in media and entertainment in an article in *Life* magazine on 4 April 1949 and in the publication *Red Channels: The Report of Communist Influence in Radio and Television*, issued in 1950 by the right-wing journal *Counterattack*. Copland had to testify before McCarthy's Senate committee in late May 1953.[14] That summer the State Department refused to renew Bernstein's passport because of his political sympathies, a potential death blow to his conducting career. Bernstein hired Jim McInerney, once head of Criminal

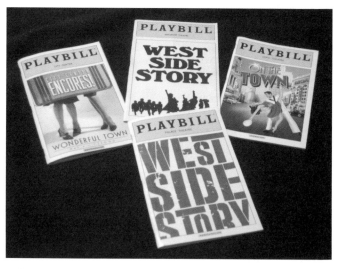

Evidence of Bernstein's musicals in New York revivals (*clockwise from left*): *Wonderful Town* at City Center Encores! (2000), *West Side Story* at Minskoff Theatre (1980), *On the Town* at Lyric Theatre (2014–15), *West Side Story* at Palace Theatre (2009–11).

Investigation for the Department of Justice, who helped clear his name. Bernstein had to sign a lengthy, humiliating affidavit dated 3 August 1953 in which he minimized his participation in many of the groups with which he had been associated and stated that he never had been a Communist, and that, indeed, 'My religious training and belief would necessarily make me a foe of communism.'[15] In a letter to his brother, Bernstein spoke candidly: 'It was worth the whole ghastly & humiliating experience just to know him [McInerney], as well as the $3,500 fee. Yes, that's what it costs these days to be a free American citizen.'[16] Bernstein was more fortunate than his friend Jerome Robbins, forced to testify before the House Un-American Activities Committee in May 1952. In fear for his career Robbins named colleagues who had been Communists. Bernstein continued to work with Robbins, but some on the left disassociated themselves from the choreographer for years thereafter.[17]

On the Waterfront and *Serenade*

Bernstein worked at Tanglewood in the summer of 1953 while awaiting his passport renewal, crucial for his autumn activities in Brazil, Italy and Israel. He spent three uninspiring weeks with the Orquestra Sinfônica Brasileira in September and then went to Israel, where Felicia joined him for two months. Bernstein conducted 21 concerts with the Israel Philharmonic in four weeks, his great popularity there remaining intact.[18] After he went to Italy with his wife for the late autumn, he did concerts in Milan and Florence, and then three different programmes with the Santa Cecilia Orchestra in Rome. One of Bernstein's most distinctive efforts as a guest conductor took place that December when he substituted for Victor de Sabata at La Scala in Milan in *Medea* by Luigi Cherubini. Soprano diva Maria Callas, singing the title role, insisted on hiring

Bernstein, who helped reinvigorate the score and increase the opera's dramatic impact, assisted by Callas's formidable interpretive powers. He was the first American conductor to work there and was invited back the following year. He flew home with Felicia for the holidays on 15 December, returning to Milan later in the month for more performances.

Upon Bernstein's return to New York in January, his intention was to dive into composing *Candide*, but Hollywood beckoned. Producer Sam Spiegel's latest project was *On the Waterfront*, directed by Elia Kazan. Bernstein's initial impulse was to refuse the project because he was busy, and also because Kazan was one of the most prominent informers for the House Un-American Activities Committee. Spiegel, however, convinced the musician to watch the rough cut, the finished film without music. Bernstein loved it, not surprisingly given the film's powerful story, memorable cinematography and wonderful performances by Marlon Brando, Eva Marie Saint, Lee J. Cobb and Rod Steiger. The resolution of Bernstein's passport episode had removed him from blacklists, so the film industry accepted him and he began work in February. Spiegel and Kazan allowed Bernstein to work unsupervised, meaning that the composer decided where to add music and how long each segment would be. He wrote 27 cues that total 42 minutes of music.[19] Bernstein did not conduct his soundtrack with the studio orchestra in California, but attended the sessions and played jazz piano for the scene when Terry and Edie are in the bar.

The film inspired Bernstein. His score to *On the Waterfront* includes music of the first rank, from the soaring love theme to wild cues underscoring the violence encouraged by corrupt leaders of the longshoremen's union, the latter demonstrated by the segment that starts with timpani at the film's opening. The main title is a Coplandesque melody for solo horn with a delicious blue note on a c', a line that embodies the sadness that main character Terry feels throughout. Anthony Bushard has shown how carefully Bernstein unified the score through such themes as the 'pain motive', heard in the first cue as Terry walks along, ready to do Johnny Friendly's bidding, which results in Joey's death.[20] That music accompanies Brando's character on his journey towards self-respect as he falls in love with Joey's sister and decides to testify before the crime commission and confront Johnny Friendly. Bernstein memorably recapitulates the film's themes in Terry's tortured walk at the close. The score for *On the Waterfront* has dedicated enthusiasts and serious detractors, the fault line forming over how unobtrusive one believes that film music should be. Bernstein clearly considered himself an equal collaborator in the overall message, frequently providing music that stakes out part of the foreground. Bernstein's work on the film is powerful confirmation that he craved to bring his serious musical style to a popular medium. One could not expect him to write the same kind of music for a musical comedy, but *On the Waterfront* and *West Side Story* include material related in style, as has been pointed out by Anthony Bushard.[21]

In an essay that he wrote after finishing the film, Bernstein objected to some of his music being lost during the sound editing process, but a balanced appraisal suggests that his music received its due as sound engineers mixed dialogue, environmental noise, and music into the final product.[22] The powerful film won eight Oscars; Bernstein's work was nominated for Best Score, but he lost to longtime film composer Dimitri Tiomkin for *The High and the Mighty*. Bernstein turned some of the film's music into his Symphonic Suite from *On the Waterfront*, completed in July 1955 for its premiere that summer at Tanglewood. The suite is about twenty minutes long, mostly drawn from the film's first seven cues, with some new connecting material.[23] Despite being approached, and starting to work on such films as *Brother Sun, Sister Moon* (1972) with director Franco Zeffirelli in 1969, Bernstein never completed another film score.[24]

When Bernstein dropped everything to work on the film, he had a concert piece for solo violin in progress based on a 1951 commission from the Koussevitzky Foundation, awarded not long after the death of Bernstein's mentor. The composer made progress on the *Serenade after Plato's 'Symposium' for Violin, Strings, and Percussion* in autumn 1953, but wrote much of it during summer 1954, not long before its premiere in Venice, Italy, with violinist Isaac Stern on 12 September. It is one of Bernstein's finest concert pieces, conceived beautifully for solo violin and including music in varied styles, ranging from the composer's trademark lyricism to symphonic jazz in the final movement. An unusual aspect of *Serenade* is Bernstein's programmatic title, based upon Plato's memories of a philosophical discussion on love that involved Socrates, Aristophanes and others. Few Americans would have known the source, but a composer who had already named a symphony after an intellectual W. H. Auden poem was also willing to be stimulated by a Greek philosophical treatise while composing a violin concerto. Burton is not convinced that the *Serenade* is that closely related to the Greek philosopher, noting 'a glance at Plato reveals obvious discrepancies between Bernstein's adaptation and the original.'[25] Burton posits, for example, that the composer failed to place his movements, named after these Greek figures, in the order that the various philosophers spoke at the banquet that Plato references, and perhaps the character of some movements is not what one might expect. Shawn is more willing to take Bernstein seriously in terms of his inspiration.[26] A number of famous programmatic works have dubious relationships with their supposed models, but artistic licence can account for Burton's 'discrepancies'. It must be stated, however, that Bernstein's title hardly made it easier for the piece to become known. Part of Bernstein's inspiration might have included the homosexual orientation that is part of Plato's *Symposium*, an aspect of ancient Greek life among the intellectual elite that Bernstein probably

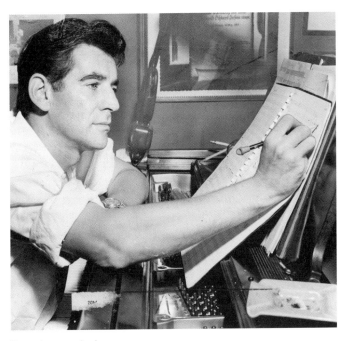
Bernstein composing in 1955.

appreciated. Bernstein used four of his *Five Anniversaries* for solo piano in writing this violin concerto, one of a number of pieces that he partially built from previous nuggets that he had composed.

The *Serenade* forms a satisfying whole. As it progresses, Bernstein bases much of what one hears on previous material, a favourite compositional method that one also hears in Copland. The opening movement, 'Phaedrus, Pausanias' (Lento, Allegro), begins with a seraphically beautiful idea with a raised fourth scale degree that reminds one of 'Maria' from *West Side Story*, and this theme would be comfortable in the sweeter moments of that show. Bernstein treats the idea in imitation through the Lento section, and then uses it to launch into 'Pausanias', the energetic Allegro full of delightful, virtuosic writing for violin. 'Aristophanes', based on two

of the *Anniversaries*, is a charming Allegretto in which Bernstein, in
his programme notes, considered the famed playwright 'a bedtime
story-teller, invoking the fairy-tale mythology of love'.[27] For the
most part the movement remains at a soft dynamic level, contrasted
by the headlong rush of 'Eryximachus', a violent *moto perpetuo*
followed by 'Agathon', the set's most elegant movement and one
of the most beautiful pieces that Bernstein ever wrote. He based
the accompaniment of the first section on the melody of the first
movement, and then provided a lyrical masterpiece for the soloist,
building to a powerful climax in the middle of the movement before
the violinist returns with a cadenza full of multiple stops that finally
dissipates before opening material returns in the strings. The final
movement, 'Socrates, Alcibiades' (Molto tenuto – Allegro molto
vivace) opens tensely, a slow section based largely on stepwise
gestures that finally resolves. Bernstein wrote similar music at
the opening of the finale to *Chichester Psalms*, there alleviating the
tension with lyricism, but in 'Alcibiades' Bernstein uses symphonic
jazz that ranges from bluesy ideas reminiscent of Gershwin to more
up-to-date references to modern jazz, including a jaunty solo for
string bass. A burst of energy in the violin leads to the closing.

Omnibus

Robert Saudek cut his teeth in the broadcasting world producing
radio documentaries, and in 1951 he became director of the Ford
Foundation's experimental television division. He launched
Omnibus in 1952, an attempt to bring highbrow culture to
television in a ninety-minute magazine show that aired late on
Sunday afternoons. Saudek's assistant producer was Paul Feigay,
co-producer of *On the Town*, who, along with feature editor Mary
Ahern, interested Bernstein in an *Omnibus* segment based on
sketches of the first movement to Beethoven's Symphony no. 5.

The musician wrote his own script, orchestrated segments from Beethoven's sketchbooks and narrated a live broadcast on the topic on 14 November 1954. With the score's first page painted on the studio's floor and musicians holding their instruments and standing on the correct lines, and other such demonstrations, Bernstein showed an intuitive talent for explaining music to the masses. His descriptions of passages that Beethoven rejected communicated real musical understanding to his general audience, using language that they understood. His twenty-minute lecture concluded with a performance of the symphony's first movement with the Symphony of the Air, formerly the NBC Symphony Orchestra. Howard Taubman expressed his appreciation for Bernstein's work soon thereafter in the *New York Times*: 'He gave his audience an insight into the mind of a creative worker. Without resorting to the rhetorical flourishes so common to discussion of good music on the airwaves, he showed what a tremendous adventure a symphony can be.'[28]

The reaction to Bernstein's first telecast was so positive that he did six more over the next four years, leading up to when he took over the New York Philharmonic's *Young People's Concerts*. His next *Omnibus* segment was 'The World of Jazz', broadcast on 16 October 1955, which included Bernstein's memorable setting of a couplet from Shakespeare's *Macbeth* to a twelve-bar blues pattern, more excellent teaching and fine playing by a studio jazz band. The programme, however, raises eyebrows today because it includes only white musicians and the major work performed is Bernstein's *Prelude, Fugue and Riffs*, which includes little improvisation, highly problematic on a show about jazz. Seven weeks later, on 4 December 1955, Bernstein's broadcast was 'The Art of Conducting', seen by an estimated audience of sixteen million.[29] The show included pithy material on the nuts and bolts of the discipline and loftier aspects of the art. On 7 October 1956 Bernstein offered 'American Musical Comedy', an informative look at the genre's musical elements and a brief tour of its history with live examples, made self-reflexive towards the end by Bernstein's call for a 'Mozart to come along' who might help the American musical theatre take its next step.[30] Given the fact that Bernstein was putting the finishing touches on *Candide* and working on *West Side Story*, he was perhaps offering himself as that 'Mozart'. Later *Omnibus* telecasts included 'Introduction to Modern Music' (13 January 1957), 'The Music of Johann Sebastian Bach' (31 March 1957) and 'What Makes Opera Grand?' (23 March 1958). Scripts and musical examples from *Omnibus* broadcasts make up most of Bernstein's first book, *The Joy of Music* (1959), and all seven of the shows have been made available on DVD. Bernstein was paid well for his *Omnibus* work and it substantially increased his personal celebrity.

Candide

Work on what would become Bernstein's third Broadway musical had to fit around his other projects. He continued conducting in Italy, including much of winter and spring 1955 working at La Scala in Milan, briefly conducting orchestras in Trieste and Florence, and leading a tour there of the Israel Philharmonic. La Scala presented Bernstein with another plum project: ten performances of a new production of Bellini's *La sonnambula* starring Maria Callas. His other work, seven performances of Puccini's *La bohème* in an old production instead of a promised new look at *Cavalleria rusticana*, was routine. In addition Bernstein was unable to interest the opera house in mounting Blitzstein's *Regina*, and he went home with no intention of returning. It was a decade before Bernstein worked in another opera house. His tour with the Israel Philharmonic included seven performances of Berlioz's *Romeo and Juliet* and his *Serenade* with soloist Isaac Stern. On this trip, Felicia Bernstein accompanied her husband for a month while carrying their son Alexander, who was born on 7 July 1955. Just a few months later, on 23 September, Bernstein's growing celebrity was on display in a television interview by Edward R. Murrow with Felicia in their apartment for the television show *Person to Person*.[31]

While working on *Candide*, Bernstein's collaborator, Lillian Hellman, suggested another project. She had translated into English a French play by Jean Anouilh, *L'Alouette* (The Lark), concerning Joan of Arc, and asked the composer to write songs for the play, which opened at the Longacre Theater on 17 November 1955. This score took the ever-eclectic Bernstein into new musical territory, drawing upon sounds of the Middle Ages and Renaissance for songs with French and Latin texts. He leavened the concoction with aspects of his recognizable musical style, writing short, charming choral works with small percussion parts. Some texts were from the Roman Catholic Ordinary of the Mass; when choral conductor Robert Shaw saw *The Lark*, he suggested to Bernstein that it could easily be adapted into a *Missa brevis*, which the composer did decades later in response to Shaw's commission.

Bernstein and Hellman began to discuss collaborating on *Candide* in autumn 1953. Hellman wrote to Bernstein with the suggestion, rhapsodizing: 'I think it [*Candide*] could make a really wonderful combination of opera – prose – songs.'[32] Simeone suggests this undated letter was sent that autumn. In a letter to Felicia from Italy on 7 February 1954, Bernstein stated that he intended to write *Candide* with Hellman, admitting that he wrote a letter refusing the project and tore it up.[33] Once Bernstein returned home he spent much of the late winter and spring composing *On the Waterfront*, with intensive work commencing on *Candide* in summer 1954 while Bernstein and family were in residence at Martha's Vineyard. Along with Hellman he collaborated with lyricist John Latouche, who was especially adept at writing satire. Sketches of the first act emerged from the summer, and work continued that autumn after Bernstein returned from his latest conducting in Italy. Bernstein and Hellman, however, broke with Latouche in November, and the two briefly considered writing lyrics themselves. Another hiatus came with Bernstein in Italy from February to June 1955, and when he returned problems with finding a lyricist continued: Dorothy Parker wrote just one song, and James Agee agreed to collaborate but died soon thereafter. Bernstein began work on *West Side Story* while they searched for another lyricist.

In December 1955 Bernstein and Hellman agreed upon Richard Wilbur, a young poet who taught English at Wellesley College.[34] He worked on *Candide* in summer and autumn 1956. Bernstein wrote to David Diamond from Martha's Vineyard on 25 May, stating that he continued to work with Hellman on the musical, but they had found Tyrone Guthrie, an English director who Bernstein said 'will save the show', and Wilbur, 'a marvelous young poet who has never written a lyric in his life, and is already doing wonders'.[35] Later in the letter, the composer noted that he also was working on the 'Romeo' show with 'a charming gifted boy named Steve Sondheim', creating 'a wild situation, even for me'.[36] Bernstein also ran off to New York to conduct, but the music for *Candide* was primarily finished by August with rehearsals starting that autumn, three weeks of try-outs in Boston and a 1 December 1956 opening.

Wilbur provided effective lyrics for the second act and cleaned up work by others in the first act. The problem with *Candide*, however, was the chasm in tone between Hellman's satirical book and Bernstein's bonbon of a score that was inspired by operetta and European models of the nineteenth century. In a letter to Copland from 29 July 1954, Bernstein noted that his inspirations for the show included Hérold and Auber, French composers of the nineteenth century, what he called a 'new wrinkle' in his work.[37] Hellman's inspiration, however, was recent and close to home: McCarthyism in the United States. She turned to Voltaire's famous novella because of its strident satire; the French writer skewered contemporary philosophers and nearly everything held significant in the 1750s. In Hellman's hands Voltaire's wide-ranging story and its sharp edge were directed at the modern world, especially in a scene where the Spanish Inquisition clearly symbolized the House Un-American Activities Committee, which Hellman had defied in testimony in 1952. It was difficult to reconcile Hellman's bitterness with Bernstein's music, which is often frothy. A further complication was that Bernstein's difficult-to-perform music necessitated that the cast be singers first, which, according to director Guthrie, complicated the presentation of Hellman's book, one of many problems the director faced.[38] Among the leads were Robert Rounseville in the title role and Barbara Cook as Cunegonde, both wonderful singers whose performances, along with those by the remainder of the cast, made for a memorable original cast recording. Reviews varied greatly, but even Brooks Atkinson of the *New York Times*, who wrote one of the few raves, noticed differences in tone between book and score: 'On the whole, Mr. Bernstein has had more latitude than Miss Hellman and has been able to make freer use of his talents. For Miss Hellman has been bound by the nature of the story.'[39] Atkinson's appreciation of the show was unusual, and the original production only ran for 73 performances.

With the original cast recording available, Bernstein's ebullient score to *Candide* became famous. Hellman never completed another version and eventually withdrew her book, but others appeared. Indeed, *Candide* perhaps has the messiest history of any Broadway musical that was commercially unsuccessful in its initial run. Its history includes the 1973 'Chelsea' production directed by Hal Prince with a new book by Hugh Wheeler that had a long Broadway run, the New York City Opera version from 1982, the Scottish Opera rendition of 1988, Bernstein's concert version from 1989 and others. Each included some different songs and numbers were moved around, and the story also changed. Helen Smith has provided a useful chapter on the show and its history, but the topic begs for a book of its own.[40]

What is it about the score to *Candide* – in whatever version a listener might know it – that has given the music such staying power? It is perhaps because here Bernstein left his usual inspirations for Broadway – blues, jazz, conventional songs for musical theatre – and allowed his eclecticism and *joie de vivre* to roam freely over a wide range of European music. This turns the score into an operetta, Bernstein's only essay in the genre, a point that has been explored by William A. Everett and Allen Shawn.[41] The rollicking Overture includes a few of the show's best themes woven into a delightful sonata form, demonstrating that what follows will be musically sophisticated.

The vocal numbers constitute a veritable musical tour. The 'Westphalian Chorale' is an updated version of homorhythmic Baroque chorale harmonizations, a style that Bernstein later parodied in 'Almighty Father' from *Mass*. 'O Happy We' opens in a tuneful 7/4, representative of one of Bernstein's favourite metres, switching to triple metre when Candide and Cunegonde reach the title text. The musical chaos of Bernstein's 'Auto-da-fé' in the Inquisition scene reminds one of Shostakovich in a rambunctious mood, with frenetic activity in the strings and wild modulations. Solo passages immediately echoed by chorus are redolent of Gilbert and Sullivan and Gershwin's *Of Thee I Sing*. In his programme notes to the 1989 recording, Andrew Porter noted that Cunegonde's 'Glitter and Be Gay' provides the nineteenth-century convention of the waltz.[42] That song with its extensive coloratura is also a parody of an operatic aria like the 'Laughing Song' from *Die Fledermaus*. Other waltzes in the score include 'The Paris Waltz', 'You Were Dead You Know' and 'What's the Use?' Other dance-like, metric schemes in *Candide* include the gavotte, appearing as the same melody in 'Life Is Happiness Indeed' and 'The Venice Gavotte'; a polka in 'We Are Woman'; a schottische in 'Bon Voyage'; and a barcarolle in 'The King's Barcarolle'. The Old Lady announces 'I Am So Easily Assimilated' in a tango, an uproarious work for which Felicia Bernstein supplied the Spanish words. Adding to Bernstein's tour of musical periods, as Porter has noted, the song 'Quiet', with its chromatic and angular melody, is a parody of twelve-tone composition. The finale, 'Make Our Garden Grow' – perhaps the most telling moment illustrating the difference in tone between Bernstein's music and Hellman's book – concludes with music that sounds frankly operatic. It is one of the most unforgettable moments in Bernstein's output, but perhaps too serious and life-affirming for a satire.

West Side Story

The most famous composition of Bernstein's life, *West Side Story* is one of the iconic works of the American musical theatre and has been considered in detail in numerous sources in terms of its creation, music and cultural significance.[43] This segment will be concerned primarily with Bernstein's role in the show's creation and describe the music and Bernstein's principle influences. Jerome Robbins conceived the idea for updating Shakespeare's *Romeo and Juliet* in early 1949 with a Jewish Romeo and Catholic Juliet and shared it with Bernstein and playwright Arthur Laurents. By May, Laurents had shown the composer a draft of four scenes of *East Side Story*, but the collaboration stalled because all three men were consumed by other projects. Bernstein returned from Italy in June 1955, supposedly ready to work on *Candide*, but he had a third idea that he presented to Laurents. They took it to Robbins, who still favoured the adaptation of *Romeo and Juliet*.[44] On Bernstein's birthday, 25 August 1955, Laurents and Bernstein were both working in southern California, Bernstein conducting in the Festival of the Americas at the Hollywood Bowl. Lounging around the pool at the Beverly Hills Hotel, they read about Mexican gangs in Los Angeles and realized that gang wars between Puerto Rican and white youths on Manhattan's West Side might give them a background for the project. Robbins liked the idea, inspiring Laurents and Bernstein to prepare a three-act outline in September.[45]

Bernstein hoped to write the lyrics, but was too busy. Laurents knew Stephen Sondheim, a young lyricist/composer, and arranged for Bernstein to meet him. They liked each other and decided to work as co-lyricists; the first song that Sondheim heard was 'Maria'. One of Sondheim's main tasks was toning down Bernstein's overly emotional lyrics. The composer gave Sondheim full credit for the lyrics once they had finished the score. They collaborated between November and March 1956, when Bernstein had to insist that the show be mothballed because *Candide* was moving towards production.[46] Most of the first act music for *West Side Story* had been written. In April 1956 the experienced Broadway figure Cheryl Crawford agreed to produce the show in association with Roger Stevens.

Bernstein returned to work on *West Side Story* in February 1957, but they needed months to finish the music for Act 2. On 22 April Crawford, worried about the violent story, left the show. Sondheim interested his friend Harold Prince who, with his partner Robert Griffith, raised the necessary $300,000 for the production in a week. Auditions began in the spring, an arduous process because of Robbins's perfectionism; some successful actors came a dozen times. Bernstein's audition notes survive at the Library of Congress, offering fascinating glimpses into the process. When Carol Lawrence auditioned on 7 May, for example, he liked her voice but thought she was 'not quite Maria', a feeling that the original Maria obviously overcame. Larry Kert auditioned for Bernardo on 7 May and then for Tony and Riff on 16 May, finally winning the role as Tony in a joint audition with Carol Lawrence.[47] Robbins insisted that every member of the cast be a dancer first, except for those playing Tony and Maria, giving Bernstein and Sondheim a challenge in teaching them the difficult score. The two took charge of that

Production of *West Side Story* at the Starlight Theatre in Kansas City at the moment when Bernardo separates Maria from Tony and orders her home.

task during the eight weeks of rehearsals from June to early August. Several cast members have spoken about how kind Bernstein was and how much he helped them with the music, a stark contrast with Robbins, whose rehearsal style was confrontational.[48] Bernstein's other major tasks during the rehearsal period included revisions and composing additional material as needed, in addition to supervising orchestrations, offering detailed suggestions to Sid Ramin (Bernstein's boyhood friend) and Irwin Kostal, and proofreading their work once it was drafted.[49] Bernstein retained the lead orchestration credit for the show. *West Side Story* played at the National Theater in Washington, DC, to packed houses for three weeks and then ran for two weeks in Philadelphia. It changed little during the try-outs, opening in New York on 26 September 1957, running for 732 performances, touring for a year and then returning to Broadway for another 249 shows.

Bernstein approached the score as an organic unit, using various motives to tie together songs and underline the show's

Production of *West Side Story* at the Starlight Theatre in Kansas City during 'Tonight', on the fire escape, the equivalent of Juliet's balcony.

principal dramatic themes. He did this in earlier shows, but the tendency is more pronounced here. The intervals of the tritone and minor seventh make numerous, significant appearances, and rhythmically the short-long treatment of the word 'somewhere' assumes structural importance. Bernstein's stylistic palette here includes several types of Latin American music and references to multiple types of jazz. The 'Prologue', which went through numerous versions, is filled with jazz references and major/minor triads, a strong dissonance that perhaps describes gang violence. The 'Jet Song' opens with the tritone and the accompaniment includes striking rhythmic complexity. 'Something's Coming', an 'I want' song that helps define Tony's character, includes Bernstein's unpredictable rhythms. 'Maria', in the style of a Broadway ballad, features rumba (3+3+2) rhythms in its bass line. When he sings her name the first time, the tritone becomes identified with her character and their all-consuming love. 'Tonight' is a beguine, based upon a dance type from Martinique, and was the third choice for the 'balcony scene' on the fire escape; 'Somewhere' and 'One Hand, One Heart' had previously been in that song placement.[50] 'America', based on constant alternation between 6/8 and 3/4, opens with a *tempo de seis*, based on a Puerto Rican model, and then launches into a Mexican *huapango*. 'Cool' is a musical pun on 'cool jazz', including the musical sounds and instrumentation of that style, especially with prominent use of flute and vibraphone. The song and subsequent dance are musically sophisticated, especially the fugal section. 'One Hand, One Heart' is a sweet, slow waltz, a tune originally in the score to *Candide*. The 'Tonight Quintet' is a contrapuntal tour de force based on operatic models, preparing the mayhem of 'The Rumble', which includes music like one might hear in a violent ballet by Stravinsky. 'I Feel Pretty' is reminiscent of an Aragonese *jota*, a Spanish song type in a fast triple metre. 'Somewhere' includes the show's most important statement of the ascending minor seventh in the opening text 'There's a', introducing one of Bernstein's most sublime melodies. The ensuing dream ballet encompasses several different types of music. 'Gee, Officer Krupke', another refugee from the *Candide* score, is a vaudevillian romp that provides comic relief and pointed satire directed at the criminal justice system. 'A Boy Like That' and 'I Have a Love', which conjoin, are in powerful contrast. The first is violent and dissonant, allowing Anita to tear into Maria for her perfidy, and Maria's answer is simple and lyrical, a response so definitive that Anita can do nothing but agree. Bernstein wanted to set Maria's final speech to music but did not succeed; she offers her reproach to everyone without even musical underscoring.[51] The finale, which underscores the procession with Tony's body being carried by both gangs, is a contrapuntal combination of 'Somewhere' and 'I Have a Love'. Bernstein played only a minor role in preparing music for the film of *West Side Story*. Its release in 1961 and subsequent great acclaim accounts for much of the show's fame.

Prominence in the New York Conducting Scene

As Barry Seldes has suggested, Bernstein's efforts to clear his name so that he could renew his passport in 1953 probably rehabilitated him with those who blacklisted him, perhaps helping to make possible his growing conducting career in the United States.[52] A notable improvement occurred in his home city, beginning with the Symphony of the Air. Bernstein conducted six concerts with the ensemble at Carnegie Hall during 1955–6, starting in November with his beloved Symphony no. 2, 'Resurrection' by Mahler and Copland's *Canticle of Freedom*. His older friend thought that Bernstein gave his work short shrift in terms of rehearsal time. The two men got over this disagreement, but they were no longer intimate friends. The orchestra at this time became embroiled in a political scandal with several members accused of being Communists. Although some tried to link Bernstein to this case, it did him no damage, possibly owing to the efforts of his new friend, Massachusetts senator John F. Kennedy.[53]

Dimitri Mitropoulos had been music director of the New York Philharmonic since 1951, but it was not a felicitous collaboration between conductor and orchestra, and Bernstein started to be regarded as a possible replacement for his friend. The *New York Times* reported on 16 October 1956 the Philharmonic's announcement that Bernstein would become co-conductor with Mitropoulos for the 1957–8 season at the Greek maestro's request, who stated his desire to pursue other opportunities.[54] The Philharmonic hired Bernstein to lead four weeks of concerts in December 1956 and January 1957, a stint that became longer when he replaced Italian conductor Guido Cantelli for a series of programmes in mid-December. Cantelli had died in a plane crash on 24 November, perhaps removing one of Bernstein's primary competitors for the Philharmonic's directorship.[55]

With his conducting, television and Broadway careers each flourishing, Bernstein was more famous than he had ever been. He was the cover story on *Time* magazine on 4 February 1957 with an article entitled 'Wunderkind', which praised him but was also critical, suggesting that his work to this point was superficial: 'At 38, Bernstein must tell himself that his talents have so far produced great excitement but no great works.'[56] At the time Bernstein was on vacation in Cuba with Felicia and Marc Blitzstein, and upon his return he took over the Philharmonic's *Young People's Concerts* and signed a contract for CBS-TV to broadcast four per year at noon on Saturdays. He also entered into negotiations to take over the orchestra's music directorship starting in the 1958–9 season, signing a contract on 3 August 1957 while embroiled in final work on *West Side Story*.[57] In published reports Mitropoulos was satisfied with his replacement, personally announcing it on 17 November 1957.[58] Mitropoulos's biographer William R. Trotter states that the younger conductor's politicking for the position included telling influential people about Mitropoulos's homosexuality, while Bernstein had masked his own sexuality with wife and children.[59] How much Mitropoulos really wanted out of the job and how much Bernstein's reported betrayal of his mentor hurt the Greek musician's reputation in New York cannot be known, but if Bernstein did anything like what Trotter suggests, it was one of the more ruthless moments of his life and helped him embark on his most significant institutional affiliation.

5

'I'm going to be a conductor, after all!': Philharmonic Maestro, 1957–69

Leonard Bernstein's life changed profoundly when he accepted the musical directorship of the New York Philharmonic.[1] It provided the only stable decade of his career in terms of employment and expectations, and contributions that he made as conductor and artistic administrator of this prominent orchestra are an important part of his legacy. To this point he was primarily known as a guest conductor, television commentator and composer of Broadway shows and other works. His concerts, television work and recordings with the Philharmonic became a large part of making Bernstein one of the most famous people in the country; in fact, those who listen to classical radio stations decades after he left the orchestra often still hear 'That was Leonard Bernstein leading the New York Philharmonic in . . .', demonstrating the continued importance of his extensive recording catalogue with the ensemble.

Acceptance of the Philharmonic directorship necessarily meant that Bernstein was turning his back on composing for the time being. He signed an initial three-year contract and then another for seven years that included a sabbatical during the 1964–5 season. Between designing seasons, conducting rehearsals and concerts, writing and broadcasting *Young People's Concerts* and other television programmes, extensive touring and recording, other administrative duties and guest conducting, there was little time to locate his inner composer, let alone actually write music.

In these eleven years Bernstein squeezed in the composition of Symphony no. 3, 'Kaddish', and *Chichester Psalms*. It was a gap that Bernstein keenly felt, and the main reason that he gave for leaving the Philharmonic in 1969, but this was a revealing decade for Bernstein concerning his lifelong wrestling match between composer and performing musician. Bernstein was a successful and charismatic conductor, and it was clearly much easier for him to lead performances than to write new works. The Philharmonic and other orchestras got in the way of his creativity, and this plagued him, but between 1958 and 1969 he had a productive excuse for his lack of composition.

Directing the Philharmonic: An 'Educational Mission'

The orchestra that hired Leonard Bernstein as their first American-born and youngest music director had forged a proud history. Founded in 1842, the Philharmonic was the oldest orchestra in the United States and one of the oldest in the world – the symphony orchestra as a continuing musical institution within a particular city is a comparatively recent phenomenon. The Philharmonic grew out of New York's large community of German immigrants. The ensemble drew from among the world's most prominent musicians for its music directorship, including, for example, Anton Seidel (1891–8), Gustav Mahler (1909–11), Willem Mengelberg (1922–30) and Arturo Toscanini (1928–36). Bernstein's predecessor, Dmitri Mitropoulos, was another outstanding conductor, and although nobody ever questioned his musicianship or dedication to his craft, some felt that he was not the best steward of the ensemble's sound or standards of precision. The orchestra that Bernstein co-conducted with Mitropoulos in 1957–8 and then took over in autumn 1958 appears to have been in need of a morale-booster and musician who would insist on world-class standards of playing.

Bernstein immediately began this process, starting with exacting rehearsals on music that the orchestra had been playing for years. This initially caused resentment, but the conductor also showed the musicians that he could be a friend and *Mensch*, cultivating relationships with men in the orchestra as individuals and offering personal loans when necessary. He repositioned the orchestra on the Carnegie Hall stage, added risers to help with balance and brought an expertise for twentieth-century music unlike anything that even the long-time members of the Philharmonic had ever experienced. These factors, combined with growth in the number of performances (from an average of 131 under Mitropoulos to 192 per year by the end of Bernstein's tenure[2]), recordings and appearances on television – which increased take-home pay – helped the orchestra to accept Bernstein and realize that this young maestro, whom they had watched mature from their assistant conductor since 1943–4, was looking out for their best interests.

Of the many descriptors that can be applied to Bernstein – composer, conductor, pianist, celebrity, recording artist, television personality – one that ties them all together is *teacher*. His family members often told the press that he never stopped teaching, easy to believe when one considers Bernstein's public persona. His father wanted him to be either part of the family business or perhaps a rabbi, and Bernstein achieved the latter: rabbi means 'teacher'. His favourite topic was music in all its forms rather than explicating Jewish scriptures, and his classroom was wherever he found himself. Bernstein's work as a public educator on television while music director of the Philharmonic will be considered below, but his entire time with the ensemble can be described in these terms. Bernstein called the position an 'educational mission'.[3] We will explore that calling in four areas of endeavour: programming strategies, touring, television broadcasts and recordings.

Programming Strategies

Bernstein began by revamping the Philharmonic schedule.
Thursday night performances were now less formal 'Preview
Concerts', with comments from the stage by the conductor and
perhaps stopping the orchestra during a piece, as in a rehearsal,
and critics were excluded. The conductor modelled a new uniform
for those performances with a Nehru jacket, but this soon was
jettisoned. Bernstein made comments from the stage on Thursday
nights but never stopped a composition in midstream; guest
conductors treated the evenings as regular concerts.[4] The
Philharmonic invited reviewers to Friday afternoon performances
of the same programme. During Bernstein's tenure Saturday
evening performances became more frequent and part of the
regular subscriptions, and Sunday concerts tended to include
lighter works and soloists of less consequence. Bernstein's initial
three-year contract called for him to lead eighteen weeks of concerts
– less than half of a season. Clearly he did not intend to dominate
the podium; indeed, during the 1960s the Philharmonic hired three
times as many guest conductors as it had during the 1950s. In an
ambitious programme to help train young conductors, and perhaps
prompted by the fact that Bernstein started his career in such a
position, the Philharmonic hired three assistant conductors for each
season, including such future luminaries as Claudio Abbado and
Edo de Waart.

Bernstein's programming plans took on a strong educational
cast, including celebration of composer anniversaries and
explorations of genres and various repertories. As the conductor
stated in the announcement of his appointment in the *New
York Times*:

> The function of the orchestra has to be different – because it is in
> New York, the center of the musical world. The programs should

add up to something: they should have a theme running through them. Programs should be built not singly, but in series, cycles, blocks. Each series, cycle, block should be a festival of a particular composer, or a particular time or a particular movement. There should always be a sense of festival about going to the Philharmonic.[5]

His first season included recognition of the bicentenary of Handel's death and the next year he memorialized the centenary of Mahler's birth with a number of performances along with guest conductors Bruno Walter, who had worked with Mahler as a young musician, and Dimitri Mitropoulos, also an important interpreter of the honoree's music. Another major festival was a two-season exploration of twentieth-century symphonic music from 1965 to 1967, when all but one of the thirty concerts that Bernstein conducted included a major contemporary symphony or concerto.[6] Other celebrations demonstrated the Philharmonic's expanded summer workload: Bernstein deputized his friend Lukas Foss to lead a festival of French and American repertories in 1965 and a tribute to Igor Stravinsky in 1966. Although it was not an area that interested him as a composer, Bernstein led an exploration of avant-garde music during the 1963–4 season, a controversial exercise that earned him praise and critical brickbats, but it was an unusual effort among major American cultural institutions during the 1960s.[7] For his final two seasons at the helm, Bernstein went all out. The 1967–8 season was the Philharmonic's 125th and included premieres of 25 commissioned works, and the concerts for his final season, 1968–9, featured public favourites from Bernstein's decade of directorship.

Bernstein seemed especially determined to increase his audience's awareness of the American symphonic repertory, starting with an ambitious sprinkling of works in his first season, choosing pieces by earlier American composers Henry F. Gilbert (1868–1928), Arthur Foote (1853–1937) and George Chadwick (1854–1931), along

Bernstein on television in the 1950s.

with many later works. During his Philharmonic tenure, almost one-third of the pieces that Bernstein conducted were by American composers, and the total of American works on all Philharmonic programmes while he was music director rose to 15 per cent. He showed special attention to pieces by Copland, William Schuman, David Diamond, George Gershwin and Charles Ives, and to his own music, but many American composers benefited from Bernstein's enthusiasm for music from his own country.

Touring

While on tour with the Philharmonic, Leonard Bernstein was a bit like a hyperactive boy running between his toys on Christmas morning. In odysseys that might last for ten weeks, the conductor routinely led the majority of the concerts, participated in numerous interviews and other publicity events, fitted in some sightseeing and then after concerts would go out and experience the nightlife. Accounts of these journeys leave little doubt that Bernstein loved touring and understood the power of publicity.

Before Bernstein even assumed the title of music director he helped lead the Philharmonic on a seven-week tour from late April to June 1958 through Latin America representing the u.s. Government, funded by President Eisenhower's Special International Program for Cultural Presentation. The itinerary included 38 concerts in 21 cities in twelve different countries;[8] Bernstein conducted the first 21 concerts and then split the remainder with Mitropoulos. American vice president Richard Nixon was also travelling through the region at the same time, and he gave a joint press conference with Bernstein in Quito, Ecuador. The Philharmonic's reception throughout their tour tended to be that of conquering heroes, but Nixon was greeted with hostility in a region that often feels ignored or manipulated by the United States. The Philharmonic had tight control over what was reported back home, but its rapturous receptions included multiple, packed concerts in La Paz, Bolivia, at a time when the country had just experienced a minor, bloodless coup and similar success in Bogotá, Colombia, when there was an election with corresponding political violence.[9] Felicia Bernstein accompanied her husband for a good part of the tour and had the special pleasure of seeing his popular concerts in Santiago, where she grew up.[10]

On 3 August 1959 Bernstein and the Philharmonic left on a ten-week journey through Greece, Lebanon (without the Jewish Bernstein, thought to be too big a target), Turkey, the Salzburg Festival in Austria, Poland and three weeks in the Soviet Union, and returned with concerts in Luxembourg, France, Switzerland, Yugoslavia, Italy, Norway, Finland, Sweden and Great Britain, fifty concerts performed in 29 cities in seventeen countries. A substantial tome could be written just concerning the time spent in the Soviet Union. This tour, ending in Washington, DC, on 12 October, was also sponsored by the Special International Program for Cultural Presentations.[11] Bernstein led 36 of the concerts, dividing conducting responsibilities with Thomas Schippers and Seymour Lipkin, a pianist who also played the solo part in Bernstein's Symphony no. 2, 'The Age of Anxiety', in seven concerts. Each performance included an American work.[12] As the tour proceeded behind the Iron Curtain, the Philharmonic was a smash in Warsaw, generating a forty-minute ovation at the final concert. Bernstein finally sent the orchestra off stage and returned to play solo piano pieces, including Chopin, for the Polish crowd.

The portion of the tour in the Soviet Union was unforgettable for Bernstein. There were eight concerts in Moscow (five at the beginning of the visit and three at the end), six in St Petersburg and four in Kiev. Bernstein had learned some Russian before the trip and used it to speak from the stage (his longer talks were translated), a practice that was highly unusual in the Soviet Union. After the first visit to Moscow, he was pressured to stop.[13] During the first week Bernstein led the five concerts in the elegant hall at the capital's Tchaikovsky Conservatory; the first, on 22 August, opened with a brisk reading of the Soviet national anthem followed by his performance of Mozart's Piano Concerto in G, K. 453, with Bernstein conducting from the keyboard, an uncommon act in the Soviet Union. The concert also included Samuel Barber's Essay no. 2 for Orchestra and Dmitri Shostakovich's Symphony no. 5, the latter sending the audience into frenzied applause. Bernstein was 'called back dozens of times to take bows. He received bouquets. He threw kisses to the audience and then, following the Russians' custom, he began to applaud with them.'[14] He led the orchestra in two encores. Other repertory from this first week included Bernstein's own Symphony no. 2, 'The Age of Anxiety'; *The Unanswered Question* by Charles Ives, a brief, philosophical work that Bernstein explained from the stage in English with an interpreter, repeating the work following the audience's positive reaction; and the Concerto for Piano and Wind Instruments and *The Rite of Spring* by Stravinsky, the latter with extra musicians drawn from the Moscow Symphony.[15] Stravinsky's famous ballet was considered decadent by Soviet authorities and played sparingly there. The composer's piano concerto with winds had never been heard in the country.[16] The *New York Times* reported that after the concerto 'The thunder of applause and shouts of bravo that burst forth . . . were deafening.'[17] Bernstein's championing of Stravinsky, who had not visited his native land for several decades, helped pave the way for the Russian composer's visit to the USSR three years later.

The remainder of the trip included a great deal of memorable music-making along with Bernstein's efforts to meet Boris Pasternak, author of *Dr Zhivago*, who was no friend of the Soviet government. Felicia Bernstein went to the area where the writer lived and had a chance meeting with him. The Bernsteins dined with Pasternak and he attended the Philharmonic's final concert in Moscow. The conductor took his television activities on tour, taping a programme for American audiences on points of similarity between Copland's *Billy the Kid* and Shostakovich's 'Leningrad' Symphony no. 7, offered in English before a clueless Russian audience. Bernstein's father Samuel had chosen not to accompany his son on this trip, but Bernstein met his uncle and called Samuel so the brothers could speak, inspiring his father to fly there.[18] After leaving the Soviet Union, the Philharmonic pushed on for another month in Europe on both sides of the Iron Curtain, finally performing in London, where British critics took issue with Bernstein's energetic conducting. The travelling party then flew to Washington, DC, to perform before representatives of the American government and ambassadors from each nation on the tour.

The visit to the Soviet Union revealed much about Bernstein, who believed that he could open doors and soften political differences through music. His programming was calculated to draw attention. His overtures to Pasternak were controversial, but Bernstein often used his celebrity to meet interesting people or attempt the unusual. Some of the Soviet response was critical. Music critic Aleksandr Medvedev, writing for *Sovetskaya Kultura*, published by the Cultural Ministry, savaged Bernstein's habit of speaking from the stage and lampooned his repetition of *The Unanswered Question* after what he called 'a ripple of cool applause' from the audience, a misrepresentation of what transpired in the hall. Medvedev went on to criticize the conductor for a crusade that he called 'Leonard Bernstein is Lifting the Iron Curtain in Music'.[19] As Burton suggests, there was some truth in this remark. The musician craved the large stage throughout his life. He probably did want to help end the Cold War. After being mobbed by members of the Russian audience after concerts and often recognized in the streets, Bernstein remarked: 'I feel we are this much closer. Nothing else will be worth a hill of beans if we don't have peace.'[20] He was becoming the master of the grand gesture that he could make because he was Leonard Bernstein, many of which occurred in his later life: his Viennese triumphs, especially championing the music of Mahler, a Jewish musician, bringing what he saw as Jewish music to a city with a history of anti-Semitism; conducting works by composers popular in their home countries, accomplished many times in Vienna but also in the Soviet Union, Germany, France, England and elsewhere; his revealing and grandiose Symphony no. 3, 'Kaddish' (1963); the flashy statement that was his *Mass* (1971); and bringing together musicians from several nations into an orchestra to perform Beethoven's Symphony no. 9 in Berlin in December 1989 after the Wall had come down. It takes a strong sense of self, an appreciation of historical trends and an understanding of the power of perception to coordinate such actions.

Bernstein continued to tour with the Philharmonic even past his tenure as music director, forging a legacy that can only be hinted at here. Following the 1959–60 season, he took the orchestra to Japan for three concerts of contemporary music in Tokyo as part of the East–West Encounter, and then a tour of six cities with more conventional repertory, including his Symphony no. 1, 'Jeremiah'. That visit included an opportunity for the 25-year-old Seiji Ozawa, a Bernstein protégé, to conduct in his own country. Over the next fifteen years or so there were many more tours, including a splashy 32-concert odyssey celebrating the American Bicentennial and featuring an all-American programme that started in Carnegie Hall on 20 May 1976, thirteen concerts in eleven European cities in seventeen days in June, and a final blow-out on 4 July at Central Park's Sheep Meadow before a huge crowd.[21] Few knew that this tour was also a display of his ability to compartmentalize his professional and personal lives: as will be described in Chapter Six, during this tour Bernstein was in the midst of a contracted and painful break-up with his wife Felicia over his desire to live as a gay man in a changing world.

Television Broadcasts

The conductor who moved into the Philharmonic directorship in autumn 1958 was already known for his segments on *Omnibus*, so it seemed inevitable that Bernstein and the orchestra would become joint stars of the small screen. The broadcasts aimed at adult audiences lasted only until 1962 because of sponsorship issues and Bernstein's realization that they took too much of his time, but the *Young People's Concerts* started in the winter of 1958 before he became music director and lasted until 1972, three years after he left the orchestra. At this point Bernstein's 53 broadcasts aimed at thirteen-year-olds have become described in a book, several biographies and numerous theses and dissertations.[22] The man possessed a special talent for explaining music to people who knew nothing about it, and the programmes reached not only the adolescent audience, but younger children and adults as well. Many musicians have said that the broadcasts were strong influences on their desire to pursue a career in the art. The *Young People's Concerts* form a unique legacy in the history of American music education and constitute one of television's true successes in the area of cultural education.

Bernstein and the composer confer on the score for Aaron Copland's *Connotations* before its premiere at Philharmonic Hall in New York City, September 1962.

David Geffen Hall at Lincoln Center in New York City, originally opened as Philharmonic Hall in 1962 during Bernstein's tenure as music director of the New York Philharmonic.

The *Young People's Concerts* were not creations of nameless underlings with Bernstein rushing in at the last moment to provide star power; he was active in every aspect of the project. He drafted the scripts on yellow legal pads, the originals of which survive in the Bernstein Collection at the Library of Congress. He then took the scripts to his committee of editors, which included series director Roger Englander and Broadway composer and children's author Mary Rodgers (daughter of Richard Rodgers), among others, who helped Bernstein edit them for his target audience. Changes went on until broadcast time, and close attention had to be paid to the timing of script and musical examples so that the broadcast would fit into the exact timing that the network allotted for a one-hour programme with space for advertisements. Bernstein eventually moved from using a typescript to a teleprompter, but he always looked natural in front of the camera, combining his good looks and Harvard elocution with wit and enthusiasm. He easily transitioned between speaking, playing examples at the piano (sometimes while singing) and conducting, cueing the orchestra virtually in a single motion when he mounted the podium. When the broadcasts first started they were televised live in the middle of a Saturday, moving to prime-time broadcasts for six years in 1961, and returning to Sunday afternoons late in the run. Videotaping of the shows started in March 1960, and with the new technology Bernstein did each show twice, once as a rehearsal, before two different audiences. Bernstein usually did four such broadcasts per year, even through his sabbatical season of 1964–5. The *Young People's Concerts* corresponded with his three children's childhoods, giving Bernstein models at home that helped him to know what might interest young people.

It was a question from his daughter Jamie that caused Bernstein to create the 36th programme, 'What is a Mode?', broadcast on Wednesday 23 November 1966. She was encountering difficulties in finding chords for a Beatles song on her guitar and asked her father, who explained that the song is modal, making the harmonies slightly different. As his explanation progressed, she suggested that he turn it into one of the *Young People's Concerts*. As was usually the case, he formed the title as a question, which he answered by lecture and example over about fifty minutes. He starts 'What is a Mode?' by explaining major and minor scales, and then plays 'Fêtes' from Debussy's *Nocturnes*, a modal work that also closes the broadcast so that the audience could hear how much they might have learned. He framed every programme with one work, systematically building the audience's knowledge of the day's topic before the repetition. His exploration of modes progressed through Dorian, Phrygian, Lydian and Mixolydian with many examples, both from the piano and with orchestra. Aeolian, the same as a pure minor scale, and Locrian, which he terms 'unsatisfying' and represented by few musical works, he dismisses quickly, and moves briefly to the Ionian mode, represented by the C major celebration that is the last thirty seconds of Beethoven's Symphony no. 5. Bernstein then returns to Debussy's 'Fêtes', this time providing musical examples and identifying which mode one hears in each melody. Whether or not members of the audience might actually identify each mode is somewhat questionable, but most members of the audience at least know that they are listening to alternative scales and have an idea of their typical emotional and musical associations.

An excellent example of the charm that Bernstein brought to the *Young People's Concerts* may be seen in his discussion of Mixolydian mode. After conducting the 'Polonaise' from Act III of Mussorgsky's *Boris Godunov* as his final example of Lydian, he sits at the piano and introduces the sound of Mixolydian, encouraging the audience to clap when they hear 'the one odd note'. He then states that jazz and Afro-Cuban music make frequent use of Mixolydian, playing a typical Cuban riff. Then to the delight of the audience he plays one phrase of 'My Baby Does the Hanky Panky' (popularized by Tommy James and the Shondells in 1966) and more of 'You Really Got Me' (The Kinks, 1964), singing along with both tunes. The audience applauds, obviously enjoying the spectacle of the Philharmonic music director pounding out some rock 'n' roll. Bernstein then plays a snippet of 'Norwegian Wood' (The Beatles, 1965), emphasizing the lowered seventh scale degree as he has in other examples. He moves to a short excerpt from Debussy's *The Sunken Cathedral*, drawing a sonorous sound from the instrument's lower range. His orchestral example is the 'Danzon' [*sic*] from his own *Fancy Free*, perhaps a bit self-serving, but it is a jaunty excerpt that returns the audience to his original point with the mode concerning Cuban music and concludes an effective, popular explanation of Mixolydian mode.

In a continuation of the type of programming that Bernstein had done on *Omnibus*, his television schedule with the Philharmonic included shows pitched to an adult audience from 1958 to 1962, sponsored by the Ford Motor Co. His first *Lincoln Presents* broadcast was on 30 November 1958, followed by a *Young People's Concert* on 13 December, and then three more presentations of *Lincoln Presents* from January to March 1959, each an original script that delved into material at a deeper level than he could for children. There were eleven more broadcasts, now under the title *Ford Presents*, broadcast between October 1959 and March 1962, varying between programmes based around Philharmonic visits to Moscow, Venice, Berlin and Japan and explorations of topics such as 'Rhythm', 'Romanticism in Music' and 'The Drama of Carmen'.[23] Ford then withdrew its sponsorship and Bernstein decided to move on, writing his friend David Diamond that, although the shows were 'immensely satisfying and creatively rewarding', he felt they had taken too much of his time that he should have been using for composing.[24]

An effective example of these shows is 'Romanticism in Music', aired on 22 January 1961. The difference in intent between this and a *Young People's Concerts* is clear. Bernstein ranges beyond musical concerns and assumes considerable prior knowledge, or at least his audience's willingness to accept the broad nature of the Romantic movement. Bernstein refers to history, painting, dance and poetry, including costumed actors doing readings and dance excerpts. He places emphasis on the artist as creator and posits the 'Four Freedoms of Romanticism': tonality, rhythm, form and sonority. A comparison between the Baroque nature of 'Dido's Lament' from Purcell's *Dido and Aeneas* and Isolde's death music from Wagner's *Tristan and Isolde* is especially revealing, and other musical examples – with piano, the New York Philharmonic and singers – include a Chopin nocturne, excerpts from Berlioz's *Romeo and Juliet* and Verdi's *Aida* (the latter featuring Leontyne Price), the Act III quartet from Wagner's *The Mastersingers of Nuremberg* and Richard Strauss's tone poem *Don Juan*. It was an extraordinary show to have appeared on network television.

Bernstein made himself a multimedia presence, turning the scripts from some of his shows into book chapters. As previously noted, *The Joy of Music* (1959) was based upon his *Omnibus* scripts and also included a few other essays.[25] *The Infinite Variety of Music*

(1966) primarily was scripts from his *Lincoln Presents* and *Ford Presents* broadcasts, and several of his children's programmes appeared in *Leonard Bernstein's Young People's Concerts* (1970).[26] His assistant Jack Gottlieb aided with some of these publications.

Bernstein's video career extended well beyond his activities with the New York Philharmonic, with which he also filmed a number of concerts that remain available on DVD. He filmed concerts with the London Symphony Orchestra, various performing groups in Paris, the Israel Philharmonic Orchestra and many performances with the Vienna Philharmonic. Other videos included a documentary on his trip to Jerusalem after the Six-day War in 1967, *Journey to Jerusalem*, and *The Little Drummer Boy*, his consideration of Mahler's life and music. A remarkable show that he was part of aired on 25 April 1967: *Inside Pop – The Rock Revolution*, a production of CBS News. It opened with twenty minutes of Bernstein with a piano and tape recorder, reacting revealingly to the pop songs, explaining them to his generation. Some examples he clearly likes and describes with enthusiasm and others he treats with condescension, but what other classical figure at the time was willing to address the generational musical divide in such a frank manner, showing how rock is part of an historical and musical continuum? Bernstein's embrace of the video world was unusual among classical artists at the time.

Audio Recordings

Bernstein's recording legacy with the New York Philharmonic is far too extensive to approach in authoritative detail without book-length coverage. As noted earlier, he signed his first recording contract with Columbia in early 1950 – the dawn of the LP era – and began to record with the Philharmonic as a guest conductor. In 1959 he inked another contract with the label that gave Bernstein full discretion on repertory to be recorded – an extraordinary concession

– and a guarantee of $45,000 per year in royalties. Bernstein set out recording works that were part of his Philharmonic programming and other pieces that would probably not have appeared on a subscription concert, but might sell. Working in such studio venues as the St George Hotel in Brooklyn, the 30th Street Studios and the Manhattan Center, often at night when there was less traffic, the conductor and orchestra characteristically did a number of works on a single day. On 16 February 1960 at the St George Hotel, for example, they recorded Mahler's *Songs on the Death of Children* with Bernstein's long-time friend mezzo-soprano Jennie Tourel, Prokofiev's *Peter and the Wolf* (Bernstein recorded his narration on 25 May), and Tchaikovsky's *Capriccio italien*, over 90 minutes of material (with narration) that became available commercially.[27] Detailed perusal of the Philharmonic discography shows that Bernstein recorded often with them throughout his tenure as music director, continuing in frequent sessions through the 1970s and '80s, ending in 1989 with all-Copland and all-Tchaikovsky concerts recorded live at Avery Fisher Hall in October.[28] Just the listing of works by composers of Bernstein's recorded legacy with the Philharmonic is nearly twelve pages in length and includes approximately 450 works,[29] ranking as one of the most important associations between a conductor and orchestra in the history of recording.

Like all things musical, recordings are judged subjectively by both sophisticated and inexperienced ears. Unlike concerts, however, they are a permanent part of the musical record that one can return to and study, allowing development of informed and documentable opinions. In the case of Bernstein, where his highly physical style of conducting sometimes turned off critics who had trouble paying attention to the interpretation, an audio recording leaves one with just sound and interpretation. On recordings Bernstein shows himself to have been a master in a number of repertories. Progressing chronologically, the first composer that

Bernstein seems to have had a special understanding of was Franz Joseph Haydn, especially his later symphonies, in which he captured both the grandeur and puckish humour. His extensive recordings of Beethoven, both with the New York Philharmonic and Vienna Philharmonic, boldly capture the music's intensity and excitement. Critics often faulted Bernstein's work in the Romantic era, believing that he bent pieces out of shape with inconsistent tempos to clarify his interpretation, but he understood the subjectivity and wide range of moods that mark music from the period, factors that contribute strongly to his success with Berlioz, Schumann, Wagner and Tchaikovsky. For a more circumspect composer like Brahms, Bernstein had more to learn, but his mature versions of the composer's symphonies with the Vienna Philharmonic are superb.

Moving into the twentieth century, one finds Bernstein comfortable in almost every corner except the post-war avant-garde, which he seldom recorded. Mahler was one of his finest specialities. Bernstein found him most of all a Jewish composer – despite his conversion to Roman Catholicism – and rendered his symphonies and orchestrally accompanied songs with a powerful sense of drama. He was as responsible for the resurgence of interest in Mahler's music since the 1960s as any other musical figure. Bernstein's impeccable rhythmic sense and understanding of possible orchestral colours, along with an exceptional ability at score-reading, made him a natural for Stravinsky, Bartók, Shostakovich, Prokofiev and Sibelius, and with twentieth-century American composers he had few peers in terms of the frequency with which recorded the music and the understanding that he brought to it. His mentor Copland benefited handsomely from Bernstein's love for his music and the interpretive elan that he possessed for it, but Gershwin, Schuman, Barber, Diamond, Blitzstein, Ives and other American composers were all part of the air that Bernstein breathed. He was possessive about the music that he conducted and recorded, once remarking when

conducting Beethoven: 'If I don't feel like I'm Beethoven, I'm
not doing it well.'[30] Some might call this hubris, but such was
Bernstein's commitment to his art and the way that he lived and
owned the music that he interpreted.

Bernstein and the Critics with the New York Philharmonic

If someone accepts the directorship of the local symphony
orchestra for eleven years, regular assessment of their work by
critics from the media is to be expected. In a city such as New York,
that scrutiny will be intense and, perhaps, contentious. Fond of
grand gestures and ambitious programming, Bernstein presented
a big target for critics. When he accepted the directorship, the music
critic at the *New York Times* was Howard Taubman, who publicized
the orchestra's many problems under Mitropoulos in an article that
appeared on 29 April 1956.[31] It is hardly surprising that the Greek
conductor was eased out of his position over the next few seasons.
Bernstein took over and the New York critics embraced him;
Taubman, for example, approved of his work in terms of the
orchestra's sound, programming and increase in size of the
audiences.[32] He moved to the drama critic's desk at the *Times* in
1960, making Harold C. Schonberg the head reviewer of musical
performances. His hard line towards Bernstein and his leadership
of the Philharmonic became a major story in New York's musical
circles during the 1960s. The conductor remained popular with the
audience and the orchestra flourished, but Schonberg's reviews
reflected a different reality. He disapproved of Bernstein's interpretation of works from the nineteenth century and argued that fine
individual performances were more important than organizing
seasons around themes.[33] At the end of the 1960–61 season,
Schonberg criticized Bernstein for only conducting the first six

and last six weeks of the 28-week Philharmonic season, finding that the orchestra did not play as well for guest conductors. He granted Bernstein some of his abilities, but also derided the musician as 'the classical-music equivalent of an Elvis Presley' whose concerts carry 'the aura of show business rather than music-making'.[34] Before presenting his thoughts about Bernstein's work with various repertories, Schonberg blasted him with both barrels: 'Thoughtful people are beginning to complain more and more of Mr. Bernstein's antics on the podium, just as thoughtful musicians are beginning more and more to ask if Lenny is ever going to grow up.'[35]

In April 1962 Bernstein ran into a difficult situation with his friend the pianist Glenn Gould, a brilliant, if eccentric, artist. They were performing Brahms's Piano Concerto no. 1, which Gould wanted to play more delicately than was customary and with a strikingly slow tempo for the first movement. Bernstein was unable to dissuade Gould and elected to inform the audience that artists can disagree on aspects of a performance, but they would use Gould's tempo. It was not supportive treatment of Gould, but Bernstein probably felt that his own judgement might be questioned. Schonberg's review of the concert was bizarre. Under a usual *Times* review headline he pretended that he was writing a letter, at times in intentionally poor English, to the Russian pianist and composer Ossip Gabrilowitsch (1878–1936), lampooning Bernstein's comments before the concerto and then suggesting that Gould favoured the slow tempo because of inadequate technique. He allowed Bernstein no quarter in a challenging situation: 'You know what, Ossip? I think that even though the conductor makes this big disclaimer, he should not be allowed to wiggle off the hook that easy. I mean, who engaged the Gould boy in the first place? Who is the musical director? Somebody has to be responsible.'[36] Bernstein was not blameless, but here Schonberg failed to exercise his own office in a responsible manner. He was not the only critic who often attacked Bernstein: Alan Rich, who wrote for the *New*

York Herald Tribune, was another reviewer who frequently disliked the director's podium manner and interpretations.

Allen Shawn has suggested that Schonberg was generally kinder to Bernstein after his sabbatical season of 1964–5.[37] Indeed, when Bernstein left the Philharmonic position in 1969, Schonberg allowed him a positive exit, saying that he had learned 'to conduct the big works of the repertory in a way that had shape as well as color, structural integrity as well as freedom within the phrase'.[38]

Bernstein Without the Philharmonic, 1957–69

Harold C. Schonberg more than once said that Bernstein tried to do too much in addition to leading the Philharmonic, and he did pursue an astonishing range of guest conducting and other opportunities during his forties and early fifties, including two major compositions. These experiences emerge as vignettes, coming into focus as Bernstein moves in and out of his Philharmonic duties, often rushing off for something just as demanding.

Right after *West Side Story* opened in late September 1957, Bernstein and his wife flew to Israel so that he could conduct the opening concert on 2 October for the Fredric R. Mann Auditorium in Tel Aviv, the new permanent home for the Israel Philharmonic. Still a heroic figure in Israel, Bernstein came for the first time since 1953. He shared the festivities with world-class soloists: violinist Isaac Stern, pianist Artur Rubinstein and cellist Paul Tortelier. While there, Bernstein injured his back. The orchestra presented him with a baton made from olive wood, which he used to make his conducting a bit easier with the sore back; Bernstein thereafter never returned to what had been his customary podium style without a baton.

After his gala opening as Philharmonic music director in autumn 1958, Bernstein went to Paris for his debuts with two orchestras. The two concerts with the Lamoureux Orchestra were typical for him: the first included Stravinsky's *The Rite of Spring* (with Bernstein himself paying for the seventeen extra musicians!) so that he could perform the piece in the city where it premiered in 1913, and then his almost outlandish performance of four keyboard concertos with the orchestra in a single concert: Bach's Brandenburg no. 5, Mozart's K. 453 in G, Ravel's Piano Concerto in G major and Gershwin's *Rhapsody in Blue*. Shortly thereafter he did Mahler's Symphony no. 2 with the Orchestre National de la RTF. Critical reaction to Bernstein's work in Paris was mixed, but the French musical world could hardly miss that they had been visited by a whirlwind. He then went to Parma, Italy, where he conducted the La Scala Orchestra in a concert honouring Toscanini's death the previous year. On his return home, the Philharmonic music director announced that he would do no more guest conducting during his initial three-year contract because his work in Europe had made him realize the high quality of his own orchestra.

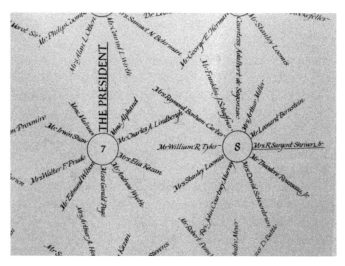

White House dinner on 11 May 1962 for French novelist André Malraux, attended by Bernstein and his wife Felicia. Detail of seating plan showing Bernstein's seat at the table next to the president.

Bernstein's theatrical activities did not completely halt while working for the Philharmonic. In May 1959 he went to London with his wife to see British productions of *Candide* and *West Side Story* before returning for a two-month summer vacation in Martha's Vineyard with his family. After its national tour, *West Side Story* reopened on Broadway on 27 April 1960, an occasion that saw the composer conduct the overture for the New York premiere. A month later, with the Philharmonic and members of the original cast, Bernstein made a recording for Columbia of the score to *On the Town*.

Bernstein became a friend of John F. Kennedy in the 1950s, and his election to the presidency in 1960 made the musician a welcome White House visitor. He was the only classical musician invited by Frank Sinatra to take part in the inauguration gala. In autumn and winter 1961–2 Bernstein attended the famous White House concert by Pablo Casals and the 80th birthday dinner for Igor Stravinsky; coinciding with both events he had personal meetings with the Kennedys. On 11 May 1962 Bernstein and his wife were at another White House dinner for the French Minister of Cultural Affairs, novelist André Malraux, where at dinner Bernstein sat between the wives of playwright Arthur Miller (Inge Morath) and Peace Corps director Sargent Shriver (Eunice Kennedy Shriver).[39] Jacqueline Kennedy approached Bernstein to serve as artistic director for the arts centre she hoped to see built in Washington.[40] Bernstein was finishing the orchestration of his Symphony no. 3 at the time of Kennedy's assassination, prompting him to dedicate the work to his friend. Two days after the president's death, on 24 November, Bernstein conducted a televised performance of Mahler's 'Resurrection' Symphony with the Philharmonic in honour of Kennedy.

Bernstein's material success became clear in 1961 when he moved with his family to a fifteen-room, two-storey penthouse at 895 Park Avenue. That autumn the film of *West Side Story* opened, a project in which Bernstein was only marginally involved, but one that significantly increased his fame and made the show and its subsequent manifestations one of his most lucrative projects. On 28 February 1962, Nina, the couple's third child, was born. Two weeks later Bernstein went to the Virgin Islands with Lillian Hellman to try and produce a better version of *Candide*, but nothing came of it. In 1962 the Bernstein family moved into their new home in Fairfield, Connecticut, their base outside of New York City for the remainder of Bernstein's life. The family spent as much time together as possible, and the couple enjoyed entertaining close friends. The composer played squash to stay in shape and in his middle age retained his appetite for psychoanalysis.

On 22 January 1964 arrived the dreadful news that Marc Blitzstein had been murdered in Martinique by three men that he had met in a bar. It was a dreadful loss for both of the Bernsteins, who considered Blitzstein one of their closest friends. Bernstein was executor for the estate and eulogized his friend at the funeral. He declared that he would complete Blitzstein's unfinished opera *Sacco and Vanzetti*, which never happened, and also referred to the composer's 'long chain of beautiful work failures', an exceedingly cruel thing to say in that situation, but Bernstein could be distressingly blunt to friends and family.[41] A triumph for Bernstein that late winter and spring was conducting Verdi's *Falstaff* at the Metropolitan Opera House, his first work there, for a new production directed and designed by his friend Franco Zeffirelli. Bernstein revelled in working with singers and orchestra in great detail, and his sensitive approach to the work even garnered a positive review from Harold C. Schonberg, who found 'Bernstein's timing and pacing surprisingly adept' and admitted that 'he knows the field as well as anybody around'.[42]

Bernstein began his sabbatical in autumn 1964. For the most part, all he did with the Philharmonic were his *Young People's Concerts*. The major composition was to be a new musical based on Thornton

Wilder's play *The Skin of Our Teeth* conceived in collaboration with Jerome Robbins, Betty Comden and Adolph Green. Bernstein's datebook from 1964 documents many meetings with these figures, especially Comden and Green, from September to the end of the year, with an intensive period at Martha's Vineyard in early October, but the collaboration fell apart in December.[43] Bernstein went with his family to Chile for the Christmas holidays and returned to New York for the New Year, still upset. On 25 January he wrote to David Diamond: 'The wounds are still smarting. I am suddenly a composer without a project, with half that golden sabbatical down the drain. Never mind, I'll survive.'[44] Some music that he wrote for *The Skin of Our Teeth* became his fine choral work, *Chichester Psalms*, written between February and June 1965. For the remainder of the sabbatical Bernstein considered another musical theatre project, spent time studying the musical avant-garde and approached a few smaller projects. He described all of this jauntily in a poetic sabbatical report to the *New York Times* the next autumn.[45]

In one of Bernstein's breaks from the Philharmonic in winter 1966 he conducted *Falstaff* for his debut at the Vienna State Opera. It was the beginning of a continuing relationship that he developed with the Vienna Philharmonic (which also plays in the opera pit) over the remainder of his career, remarkable for an American, and even more so for a Jew working in a city still known for its anti-Semitism, despite the many successful Jews who worked there in the decades before the Second World War. Bernstein enjoyed a blissful five weeks in February and March, once commenting that he was engaging in an 'illicit affair' – one of his many memorable turns of phrase that often included sexual imagery – because of his 'marriage' to the New York Philharmonic.[46] The first-class production of Verdi's masterpiece included Dietrich Fischer-Dieskau in the title role, and the premiere on 14 March received thirty minutes of applause, 48 curtain calls and ecstatic reviews. During the visit Bernstein also recorded *Falstaff* and did a concert

with the Vienna Philharmonic. He then went to London and in
the space of two weeks performed Mahler's Symphony no. 7 and
recorded Symphony no. 8 with the London Symphony Orchestra
and various choruses and soloists. (He returned that November to
tape television programmes with the London Symphony Orchestra.)
The conductor hurried back to New York to prepare the 29 April
premiere of Diamond's Symphony no. 5.

The late spring and summer of 1967 was a revealing time for
Bernstein, both in terms of his commitment to Israel and personally
to the public because of a book project that he worked on with
New York journalist John Gruen and photographer Ken Heyman
during a family vacation in Ansedonia, Italy. Bernstein was there
for concerts in Florence and Rome when the Six-day War started
on 5 June. He was then off to Vienna for Mahler's Symphony no. 2,
which the conductor used to raise money for the Israel Red Cross.
Then he assembled one of his most high-profile 'events', conducting
a concert after the war with the Israel Philharmonic, in an amphi-
theatre on Mount Scopus in northeast Jerusalem to celebrate the
city's 'liberation', obviously an Israeli interpretation. The 9 July
performance included Mendelssohn's Violin Concerto in E minor
with soloist Isaac Stern and final three movements of Mahler's
Symphony no. 2, 'Resurrection'. It was highly publicized and a
major part of the film documentary *Journey to Jerusalem*, but also
controversial given the feelings of the conquered Arabs. Allen
Shawn noted that Bernstein, perhaps far too optimistically, hoped
that the Israeli takeover of Jerusalem would result in peace with
the Arabs who lived there.[47]

Perhaps the best proof of Bernstein's exhibitionism is the book
The Private World of Leonard Bernstein.[48] In Ansedonia Bernstein
spent hours recording interviews with author Gruen while Heyman
took candid pictures and portraits of Bernstein and his family,
including such private moments as the conductor getting ready
for the day in his bathroom or outrageously mugging for the

camera. Charlie Chaplin and his wife Oona visited the Bernsteins, inspiring Heyman to document the evening in tremendous detail, including when the musician and silent film star jointly improvised an operatic scene. As Burton notes, Bernstein failed to vet the text and photos adequately before the book was published, with a predictably embarrassing result from critics who already found Bernstein an over-the-top figure. He wrote a letter to the *New York Times* repudiating aspects of the publication. Helen Coates issued Bernstein's official response, but, as Burton says, 'It is a lame defense.'[49] The musician spoke candidly with Gruen and he could not have been surprised when the author used the material. The text includes useful information from Bernstein, especially about the earlier part of his career, and it remains an important if idiosyncratic source.

Two of Bernstein's worlds came together in autumn 1967 when the New York Philharmonic celebrated its 125th anniversary. The Vienna Philharmonic marked the same birthday that year, and they visited New York in October with Bernstein and Karl Böhm splitting conducting duties. On 7 December Bernstein's orchestra celebrated with its gala, repeating what the ensemble played in its first concert, an unusual programme by modern standards that included a Hummel piano quintet with Bernstein playing his instrument. He returned to Vienna in May 1968 to conduct Richard Strauss's *Der Rosenkavalier*, a favourite work among the Viennese. Bernstein brought his own approach to the score and crafted a performance that some criticized, but it seems to have only added to his fame in the Austrian capital. He also performed with the Vienna Philharmonic, playing and conducting Mozart's Concerto in G, к. 453 and leading the city's premiere of his *Chichester Psalms*. He served as collaborative pianist with the husband-and-wife singing team of Walter Berry and Christa Ludwig in a programme of Mahler songs and also saw *West Side Story* at the Volksoper in a translation by his friend Marcel Prawy.

A revealing moment concerning Bernstein's relationship with popular music occurred when Jacqueline Kennedy convinced him to supervise music for Robert F. Kennedy's funeral on 8 June 1968 at St Patrick's Cathedral. It was a difficult task for Bernstein, who lacked the control he surely desired. One thing that he wanted to prevent was a request from widow Ethel Kennedy: popular singer Andy Williams singing 'The Battle Hymn of the Republic'. Bernstein left the final meeting believing that it would not happen, but it did, and even the conductor admitted that it was the most effective musical selection in the service.[50] As a composer, Bernstein freely accessed elements of jazz, blues and Latin American music, but he had little interest in most popular music marketed to white, middle-class listeners his own age.

Bernstein's last weeks with the Philharmonic corresponded with his father's death on 30 April 1969. It was surely a poignant moment for the musician. Sam and Jennie visited their son and his family a few times per year in New York, and the extended Bernstein family generally appears to have been close. Although his father had opposed his career in music, in all of his years of psychoanalysis Bernstein had probably deeply considered his father's role in his life. The music director changed one of his New York Philharmonic programmes to honour Sam, including his Symphony no. 1, 'Jeremiah', dedicated to his father, and Schumann's Symphony no. 2, one of Sam's favourites. It was tame repertory compared to the enormous works that marked a number of his last Philharmonic programmes: Bruckner's Symphony no. 9, Beethoven's *Missa solemnis*, Verdi's *Requiem*, and, his final performance, Mahler's Symphony no. 9.

Compositions: Symphony no. 3, 'Kaddish' and *Chichester Psalms*

The 'Kaddish' (1963) and *Mass* (1971) are among Bernstein's most personal compositions and ready demonstrations of his utter complexity. A number of his works straddle various musical genres – none more than these works – but he labelled *Mass* a 'theater piece', avoiding debate by admitting that it is *sui generis*. The 'Kaddish' Bernstein called a symphony, a genre for which the definition expanded in the twentieth century, but few works given the designation find a composer mixing this many elements. It includes three settings for soloist and/or chorus of an important Jewish prayer, said daily by observant Jews as 'both a hymn of praise and a supplication for peace'.[51] It is also the most important prayer said at the graveside. The prayer's text is primarily in Aramaic, not Hebrew. In a way, the symphony is a religious work, but the composer did not stop there. The orchestral music is some of the most powerful and varied of his career, ranging from atonality and tone rows to lovely melodic writing that might have appeared in Bernstein's Broadway musicals. The importance of the vocal parts over this orchestral melange at times makes 'Kaddish' seem like an oratorio, but then one must also consider the narration and the multiple concerns reflected in the spoken text: death, the planet's potential demise from nuclear weapons, taking God to task for a lack of attentiveness to humans, the relationship between us and God with speculation on who created whom, the impotence of a tired supreme being in an uncertain universe – and other issues. And then, with the symphony already carrying all of these levels of meaning, Kennedy's assassination occurs as Bernstein finishes the work, and he dedicates it to the fallen president. How many angles can a single work represent?

Bernstein had a great deal of trouble writing 'Kaddish'. The Koussevitzky Foundation commissioned it in 1955 to be premiered by the Boston Symphony Orchestra and Charles Munch, but at the time Bernstein was consumed with Broadway projects, and then started his Philharmonic tenure. Slow work began, including three weeks at the MacDowell Colony in June 1962. Munch, no longer directing the Boston Symphony, wanted to conduct the premiere in a visit to the orchestra in January 1964. Bernstein completed it by working in a white heat for the first three weeks of August 1963, but he thought the piece should first be premiered in Israel in December. The Boston Symphony graciously allowed this and Bernstein led it in Tel Aviv on 10 December, where it won 'prolonged applause and favourable press criticism', including from Alexander U. Boskovitch, writing for *Haaretz*, who praised it as 'a great human and artistic document' showing a 'sublime mastery of musical values and techniques that made use of all the advantages of our musical age'.[52] Writing to his sister Shirley, Bernstein wondered if American audiences would similarly understand the piece.[53] He had reason for his concern. The American premiere at Symphony Hall in Boston, where Felicia Bernstein served as the narrator, sent a noisy buzz through the classical music world with many critics commenting about what seemed an uncomfortable mixture between the strident spoken text and music, and the obvious conflation of genres. Ross Parmenter of the *New York Times* had much to say about the text, including: 'The recited part, indeed, bulked so large that it is almost as much a literary work as a musical one.'[54] He found the music

decidedly more palatable than the text, where it had a good deal of rhythmic invention. There were exciting climaxes, a number of choral passages were lovely, and always the tone paintings, as in the vision of heaven and the contrasting chilly dawn, were vivid.

'Kaddish' had its admirers, but the critical reception was mixed, and some reviewers were caustic.

Often the strongest condemnations of the narration came from conservative Christians who did not understand that Jewish traditions allow the believer to confront God, as one sees in the Book of Job. Bernstein saw a number of problems in the world in the early 1960s and called God to account. Railing against a parental figure might have reflected some feelings about his father. The symphony's message was not for everybody, but Bernstein was no stranger to controversy. He tried to work with poets on the text, including Robert Lowell and Frederick Seidel, but in the end decided that it needed to be his own words.[55] In 1977 he revised the work extensively, including the spoken text. No matter what one might think of the piece, it remains a fascinating personal glimpse into the man and his conscience. Allen Shawn suggests that if shorn of its narration, the 'Kaddish' would be 'a high point in the composer's mature output', but also admits that appreciating the 'superb music' without the spoken text might be difficult.[56]

The symphony is still performed and has been recorded several times, so it has not left the repertory, but it is a large work at a little over forty minutes that remains a difficult nut for some in the audience to crack, and expensive for orchestras to programme. He was not the only composer to combine tonal music and tone rows within a single work in the 1960s, and the music for both voices and orchestra is effective and related closely to the narration at any given moment. It is in three large sections – Invocation, Din-Torah, Scherzo – each subdivided into smaller segments. The prayer's text appears in each movement, the first time agitated, the second tranquil and finally triumphant. The harmonic arc of the symphony moves from dissonance to serenity and tonality, an overall plan that Bernstein used more than once in his concert works, such as in the third movement of *Chichester Psalms*. The anguished 'Amen' in the second movement of 'Kaddish' is striking, including aleatoric moments for the choir, dying out as the narrator asks God's forgiveness for the outburst. The 'Kaddish 2' that follows for soprano and orchestra is lovely, anticipating the setting for soprano, choir and orchestra of 'Kaddish 3', in a brilliant G-flat major. Connecting material is usually convincing, but there are places where narration does compete strongly with the music. One cannot help but wonder if the sense of the text might have been possible to project in half as many words.

Reminiscent of the 'Kaddish' in several ways, *Chichester Psalms* is a setting of three full psalms and parts of three others. It is one of Bernstein's most successful concert works and ranks as one of the most popular choral pieces by an American composer.[57] He accepted the commission from the dean of Chichester Cathedral, Walter Hussey, in December 1963, for the annual festival of Anglican choral music performed by three choirs of southern cathedrals, which was taking place in Chichester in July 1965. Bernstein could not have anticipated how he might write the work during his sabbatical. It was not until February 1965 that he arrived at his conception for the piece, several weeks after his collaboration on *The Skin of Our Teeth* had died. In three carefully organized movements, Bernstein managed to use themes that he had sketched in the 1940s and '50s, a song jettisoned from *West Side Story* and material that he had written for the recent, dead theatrical project. A combination of skill and good fortune allowed him to combine these diverse elements and set them appropriately with Hebrew psalm texts that would not have been on his mind when writing the music in its original form. Bernstein was never squeamish about reusing abandoned music, but few of his works were so dependent on previously composed music as *Chichester Psalms*. His insistence on using Hebrew texts surprised Hussey and the Anglican church musicians, but it seems hardly unusual for a Jewish composer.

Bernstein wrote the work between the middle of February and early May, sending the piano/vocal score to Hussey shortly after writing a letter on 11 May announcing the work's completion. He then orchestrated it and forwarded that in the summer. Bernstein accepted Hussey's invitation to attend the premiere on 31 July, which he turned into a visit to England with Felicia and his two eldest children. The orchestra, hired from London, did not start the difficult work until the day of the performance, but, as Bernstein reported to Helen Coates in a letter, the resonant acoustics in the cathedral ironed out the problems, and the choirs were ready.[58] The initial performance received mixed reviews, but they have had little influence on the score's long-term success. The three movements mesh beautifully and Bernstein tied the piece together with a five-note cell that, judging from the sketches of *The Skin of Our Teeth*, might have been the generating melodic snippet for that show. The cell sounds throughout the first movement and in the opening and closing sections of the finale. The first movement is in two sections: a brash, dissonant chorale setting of Psalm 108:2 and an irresistible dance-like passage in 7/4 in which the choir intones the entirety of Psalm 100. Except for a segment a little after the middle of the 7/4, all of the music in the movement was intended for *Skin*. The second movement is the more theatrical, placing in opposition Psalm 23 set to a lovely melody that Bernstein first wrote in the 1950s and became the song 'Spring Will Come Again' in *Skin*, and Psalm 2:1–4 set to music from 'Mix!', a violent song that had been deleted from the 'Prologue' of *West Side Story*. (Hussey had actually asked that the piece might include 'a hint of *West Side Story*', and Bernstein obliged him.[59]) The contrapuntal segment where Bernstein combines the two ideas is especially effective. The finale opens with a dissonant treatment of the cell, exorcizing the demons remaining from the previous movement, not unlike the opening of the last movement of the *Serenade* or sections of 'Kaddish'. This is all washed away by a sweet setting of Psalm 131 in 10/4, based upon an idea that Bernstein wrote in the 1940s. The work ends with a hushed return of the opening chorale, a setting of Psalm 133:1. In accordance with Hussey's wishes because of the small cathedral space, Bernstein scored the work for strings, three trumpets, three trombones, percussion and two harps. He also prepared a version for organ and percussion. The choir can be all-male with boy sopranos, as in Chichester, or mixed chorus.

As he had with the 'Kaddish', Bernstein stole the premiere from the commissioner and did the work with the New York Philharmonic in the middle of July; Hussey had little choice but to grant permission. Such moves were high-handed, but by the 1960s Leonard Bernstein knew who he was and what he could get away with, and, after leaving the Philharmonic, he spent the last two decades of his life pushing his own agenda, demonstrating his genius and, unfortunately, ageing with difficulty.

6

'I do know that the answer is *Yes*': Living with Fame, 1969–78

No longer tethered to the Philharmonic, Bernstein entered a period of drifting between major projects.[1] Conducting remained in his blood and he regularly engaged in huge commitments, with the major new effort being filming concerts live in such a manner that they could be shown in a movie theatre. He created a major legacy of such documents, several being memorable renditions of works presented in spectacular venues. His fondness for grand gestures had found a medium that ensured both audio and visual permanence. The major compositional projects during this period were enormous: *Mass* (1971), *Dybbuk* (1974) and *1600 Pennsylvania Avenue* (1976). The stories of their creations are convoluted, and their success was varied.

The period also included the major academic project of Bernstein's life: his Norton Lectures presented at Harvard University in autumn 1973. As was his wont, Bernstein went overboard, but in the process he exercised influence on how music is analysed. The concluding line of his final lecture serves as an effective symbol of this period in his life. His overall title was *The Unanswered Question*, based on the short philosophical composition by Ives that Bernstein clearly liked, and at the conclusion of his lectures, while admitting that he no longer knew what the question might be, he stated: 'I do know that the answer is *Yes*.' Such was the arc of the man's life. He declined projects, but he still agreed to do more than was perhaps humanly possible. He embraced conducting in a way that for most people would constitute a full-time career, but also produced compositions that many writers of music would want a year or more to create while not being bothered by other matters. And, causing difficulty in his personal life, during this period Bernstein started, perhaps more often, to pursue men he found attractive, and with more of a sense of commitment. He left Felicia in 1976 to try to live as a gay man. It did not work, and around the time that he was trying to reconcile with Felicia, she developed lung cancer and lived a painful twenty months, a fate that Bernstein blamed himself for, setting up the tragic, final chapter in his life.

Moving towards *Mass*

The next two years of Bernstein's life included many steps towards the composition of *Mass*, the large, personal work that he wrote for the opening of the John F. Kennedy Center for the Performing Arts in Washington, DC. He accepted the invitation to write it from Jacqueline Kennedy in June 1966.[2] Work on the piece almost certainly did not start until after his departure from the Philharmonic, and he did most of it in the year before the premiere in September 1971, a striking amount of it following his return from a lengthy conducting tour in Europe in May that year. The man could be a master of procrastination, and for *Mass* he almost missed the deadline.

Soon after his last New York Philharmonic concert in spring 1969, Bernstein went to Vienna to lead Beethoven's *Missa solemnis* in a performance honouring the centennial of the Vienna State Opera, demonstrating how much a part of the Viennese musical world he had already become. From there Rome beckoned, where Bernstein started work with Franco Zeffirelli on a film project concerning the life of St Francis of Assisi. A few weeks there in June and additional work with the Italian director in July in Connecticut resulted in new music by Bernstein, but they parted in October over disagreement about the script, leaving the composer to use part of what he wrote as music for the Street People in *Mass*. He also briefly worked with singer/songwriter Paul Simon that summer on music for the film project, resulting in a couplet that Bernstein asked Simon to allow him to use in *Mass*. According to Burton, Simon was unimpressed with the rock music that Bernstein wrote, but it is fascinating that there was even a momentary collaboration between two such figures.[3] Delays in construction of the Kennedy Center, which pushed the premiere for *Mass* back to September 1971, assisted Bernstein's slow compositional progress. Another potential project that ultimately bore no useful fruit was collaborating with Israeli actor Topol on adapting Bertolt Brecht's play *The Caucasian Chalk Circle* as a musical. Bernstein appears to have been casting about looking for something else exciting to work on at a time when he already had *Mass* staring him in the face.

Mass is Bernstein's most political work, and his consideration of the piece came at a time when he became more politically active. Starting in the late 1960s various events associated him with the anti-war movement. For mid-January 1970 he assembled a concert version of Beethoven's *Fidelio* with student soloists from Juilliard and the New York Philharmonic, which he considered appropriate because the opera was about political dissent.[4] Harold C. Schonberg disliked the performance, criticizing Bernstein's choice to do a concert version of the opera with the Philharmonic and the use of less experienced soloists.[5] Schonberg did give the conductor credit for a better understanding of *Fidelio* than he showed of Mascagni's *Cavalleria rusticana*, which he had recently directed at the Metropolitan Opera with stage direction by Franco Zeffirelli. That same week, on Wednesday, 14 January, Bernstein walked into a political firestorm that directly affected his life for several months thereafter, and he and Felicia faced reminders of the event the rest of their lives.

Felicia Bernstein became very active politically during the 1960s. She was the founder of the women's division of the New York Civil Liberties Union and a strong supporter of several causes. Along with other wealthy liberals in New York society, she was distressed by the treatment accorded to Black Panther members being held in solitary confinement with excessive bail on charges of possessing weapons with plans to kill policemen and attack institutions. While the organization and its history remain controversial, all of the defendants later were found innocent of the charges after an eight-month trial. A party at the Bernstein penthouse was merely one event held by members of the New York elite to raise money for the Black Panthers; there were ninety or more guests and they raised $10,000, including $2,000 from the conductor.[6] The musician arrived after a Philharmonic rehearsal when the party was already in progress, and he discussed the Black Panthers' goals and tactics with Donald Cox, the group's 'field marshal', a conversation lampooned by social editor Charlotte Curtis in the *New York Times* the next day.[7] She quoted Bernstein as agreeing with Cox by saying 'I dig absolutely,' an unusual phrase to hear from a middle-aged, rich white man. The *Times* editorial page piled on the next day, accusing Bernstein and other rich whites at the party of engaging in 'elegant slumming that degrades patrons and patronized alike'. The article also accused the rich whites of mocking the memory of Martin Luther King Jr.[8] For Bernstein the worst was yet to come, because the Black Panthers held anti-Zionist positions, and Bernstein found his apartment building and concerts picketed for weeks by Jewish and civil rights groups for his support of an anti-Semitic organization. In truth Bernstein's Zionist credentials could hardly be questioned. Among the press whom Felicia allowed to attend the event was satirist Tom Wolfe, whose vicious piece appeared in *New York* magazine in early June, accusing the Bernsteins of engaging in 'radical chic'. It was later published in a compilation of his work.[9] While Bernstein certainly made himself a broad target that day, Wolfe's essay bears little close scrutiny today because, while attacking the white liberals, he ignores the injustices perpetrated against the Black Panthers, placing the writer on a difficult side of the racial issues raised by the whole affair. Bernstein was profoundly embarrassed, but the controversy hardly stopped him from expressing himself politically, such as in *Mass* the following year. J. Edgar Hoover of the FBI took note of the event and ordered his underlings to write Bernstein letters that seemed to be from ordinary citizens, accusing the musician of turning his back on members of his faith.[10]

Controversy over Bernstein's interaction with the Black Panthers hardly slowed his conducting schedule, which dominated his life into the late spring. Following his five-week season with the Philharmonic, he arrived in London in mid-February for a tour that included five cities in as many weeks. He initiated his company Amberson Enterprise's series of filmed performances with an impressive version of Verdi's *Requiem* in St Paul's Cathedral. The future of videos of concert performances was completely unknown in 1970, but it was a medium that Bernstein and his business associates would cultivate for the remainder of his career. From London, the conductor was off to Paris, Rome, Tel Aviv and Vienna, continuing his *Beethovenjahr* with *Fidelio* on a radio broadcast with Birgit Nilsson in Rome, Symphony no. 3, 'Eroica', with the Israel Philharmonic in Israel, and then two performances of Symphony no. 9 in Vienna with the Philharmonic, filmed by Amberson to be excerpted in the CBS television programme *Beethoven's Birthday*. Upon returning to the United States, Bernstein quickly conducted the same symphony with the Boston Symphony Orchestra, a juxtaposition of a major work with two first-class orchestras within two weeks that few conductors in the world could have managed. Bernstein wrote a letter about his odyssey with the Symphony no. 9 to the Viennese music critic Franz Endler that was published in *Die Presse*, where he spoke of the 'charm' of the music and 'the child-spirit that lived in that grim, awkward, violent man'.[11]

In May he was back in Vienna for one of the highlights of his performing life, which he had prepared carefully for with his renditions in New York and Rome earlier in the year: *Fidelio* with the Vienna State Opera in the famed Theater an der Wien, where the opera had premiered in 1805. Amberson filmed rehearsals and performance excerpts of this production for the same CBS video. Bernstein enjoyed perhaps even more than his usual success in Vienna, directing a production that starred Gwyneth Jones and James King and received rave reviews.

That summer of 1970 Bernstein was back at Tanglewood, directing it in a triumvirate with Seiji Ozawa and Gunther Schuller. As heir to Koussevitzky, Bernstein gave an opening speech intended to inspire the students with what he called his mentor's 'central line' towards 'perpetual discovery, a mystical line to truth as it is revealed in the musical act'.[12] The *New York Times* printed his address. That summer at one of Bernstein's favourite places was complicated when his daughter Jamie, working as a guide, heard about her father's homosexual past, which he denied to her, blaming such rumours on those that wanted to hurt him.

Following Tanglewood, Bernstein and Ozawa took the New York Philharmonic on a tour of Japan in late summer 1970, capping a nine-month period when he got almost nothing done on *Mass*. Upon his return to the United States he heard that Roger Stevens, director of the Kennedy Center, had suffered a heart attack. When Bernstein visited him in the hospital, Stevens told the composer what he needed from him was a completed piece with which to open the new facility in September 1971. Bernstein resolved to work on it, but it would have to be around the full slate of guest conducting that he had arranged for himself through late spring 1971, including a five-week stint with the New York Philharmonic in late autumn 1970 and a long season in Europe that lasted much of the next winter and spring. On that trip he began to film Mahler's symphonies with the Vienna Philharmonic as part of what would be a complete project of the works with several orchestras, led the Viennese ensemble on a tour of twelve concerts in fifteen days, and again conducted *Der Rosenkavalier* at the Vienna State Opera and recorded it. He ensured that summer 1971 would have to be a flurry of activity on *Mass*.

Bernstein worked seriously on the piece in December 1970 at the MacDowell Colony in Peterborough, New Hampshire, setting the pattern that much of the work, like *Chichester Psalms*, came from previously composed music. According to Burton, he began to look for a director and offered the piece to Jerome Robbins and Frank Corsaro (a noted director of opera and theatre), but both turned him down.[13] Bernstein was then off to Europe, returning on 3 May 1971, soon realizing what desperate straits he was actually in if he were to have *Mass* completed in time for rehearsals to begin that summer. One of the first things he did was try to consult with Father Philip Berrigan, a prominent anti-war activist in prison in Danbury, Connecticut, where he awaited trial on charges of planning to kidnap Henry Kissinger and blow up heating tunnels in Washington, DC. Bernstein spent most of his allotted hour with the priest describing *Mass* and did not have a useful discussion, but he drew the interest of J. Edgar Hoover, who sent messages to President Nixon warning him to stay away from the performance because there would be seditious, anti-war messages in Latin, perhaps the ubiquitous 'Dona nobis pacem' that concludes the 'Agnus Dei' in the Mass Ordinary. Bernstein's FBI file continued to grow, here from a situation that sounds as though it belongs in a comic opera.[14]

Looking for help with the English lyrics, Bernstein spoke to his sister Shirley, a theatrical agent, who had a useful suggestion. One of her clients was Stephen Schwartz, lyricist/composer of *Godspell*, which opened that same month. She suggested that Bernstein see the show and meet Schwartz. Together they perused the sketches for *Mass*, and discovered that they could work together. Burton notes that Schwartz's entry into the project 'did indeed work wonders'. They began to work together with dispatch.[15]

Schwartz's memories of the collaboration are telling, and different from what Burton reports. Schwartz first met Bernstein in late May or early June. He learned that Bernstein wanted to honour President Kennedy in the work in addition to addressing multiple issues: contemporary political problems, unrest in the Roman Catholic Church and theological questions concerning the 'crisis of faith' that Bernstein mentioned often in his career. Schwartz reports that when he joined the project Bernstein had 'shards' of musical sections and ideas; a recognizable plot did not yet exist.[16] Schwartz recalls: 'I think I was able to help him structure the concept that he had in a way that had some kind of dramatic thrust.'[17] The work's loose story can be summarized as follows: the Celebrant struggles with his flock, who begin to doubt their faith and the Church's leadership, and this protagonist is gradually weighed down by more and more trappings from the established Church, symbolized by his increasingly elaborate vestments. Finally, during Communion, he throws the elements to the floor and shatters the vessels, launching into a lengthy, mad scene and finally leaving the stage. A boy in the cast rekindles faith for all by repeating material from the opening 'Simple Song', a theme that spreads throughout the hall.

Schwartz has described the flurry of work that they did on *Mass* that summer. Bernstein went out to Los Angeles to help with a *Candide* revival, and Schwartz accompanied him. Bernstein supplied music to which Schwartz quickly wrote lyrics. He remembers hiking through the Hollywood Hills running over the music in his head and trying out lyrics while being eyed by the police as a hippy because of his long hair, bare chest and surely his youth – Stephen Schwartz was all of 23 years old while working on *Mass*. They proceeded to work on the sections in order with little time for revisions. Schwartz recalls rewriting some lyrics before making the original cast recording and again prior to the run at the

Metropolitan Opera House in June 1972, but their rush in no way resembled what might have been done for a Broadway musical. As Schwartz states,

> if you are working on the simplest Broadway show . . . one would go through workshops and readings and developmental stages. Songs would be in and songs would be out and lyrics would be rewritten and revised, and that never happened with *Mass*.[18]

The piece perhaps never should have worked. Between Bernstein's procrastination and extensive conducting, the frenzied creation of the show, the score's rich eclecticism and the fact that the composer had no co-equal collaborators and resisted all attempts at editorial trimming, there was a good chance for an expensive disaster when *Mass* opened in the late summer. A number of critics disliked the work, but in general reviews were mixed.

The John F. Kennedy Center for the Performing Arts in Washington, DC, where Bernstein's *Mass* premiered on 8 September 1971.

But that was in the early 1970s. *Mass* has survived and continues to move audiences. Although Bernstein made sure that he was the primary creator, he surrounded himself with talented collaborators: Schwartz, director Gordon Davidson, choreographer Alvin Ailey, designer Oliver Smith, conductor Maurice Peress and orchestrators Hershy Kay and Jonathan Tunick, with Sid Ramin advising on the use of rock guitars and synthesizers and later orchestrating the chamber version. Roger Stevens helped Bernstein assemble a cast of over two hundred performers, which made *Mass* a behemoth, but also impressively moving in a way that some audience members obviously understood. Bernstein's mixture of classical ideas with Broadway, folk, rock and other styles at the time was controversial, but as Schwartz notes, Bernstein 'was ahead of the curve', helping to form 'the vanguard as to what has happened in classical music'.[19] Indeed, at a time in the nation's music when major orchestras play works that include the rock idiom, Broadway and film scores move fluidly between multiple styles and artists routinely cross over into other genres, Bernstein's all-embracing eclecticism in *Mass* seems prescient.

A journey through the score demonstrates how far Bernstein was willing to travel stylistically while providing a number of dramatic juxtapositions. The opening 'Kyrie Eleison', which emanated quadraphonically from four speakers, includes four different solo singers, each presenting different melodies with contrasting accompaniments, silenced by the opening chord from the Celebrant's guitar. He sings 'A Simple Song', a psalm text set to one of the composer's most beautiful melodies. These 'I. Devotions Before Mass' conclude with a jazzy 'Alleluia' that might have been sung by the Swingle Singers in the 1960s. The celebratory 'II. First Introit (Rondo)' opens with a street band and singers in 'Prefatory Prayers' that seem equal parts Sousa, Ives and other influences. This segment concludes with a 'Thrice-triple Canon' on 'Dominus Vobiscum', in nine-part, imitative counterpoint. 'III. Second Introit' opens with a delightfully jaunty setting of 'In nomine Patris' for choir and instruments, then contrasted by the restrained, dissonant chorale 'Almighty Father'. An atonal solo for oboe called 'Epiphany' follows, nearly avant-garde in flavour, setting up 'IV. Confession', which includes the dissonant and frightening 'Confiteor', a rock-based Trope: 'I Don't Know' that includes motives from the previous section, and finally the bluesy Trope: 'Easy', expressing a cynical approach to the sacrament of confession. What feels like the end of the work's first large section concludes with the orchestra's 'V. Meditation no. 1', a pleading setting that carries the feeling of the instrumental opening of the third movement of *Chichester Psalms*. The Meditation's conclusion is far more peaceful.

'VI. Gloria' includes four sections: the irrepressible 'Gloria tibi' in 5/8 for Celebrant and children's choir; the rock-based 'Gloria in excelsis' for choir; that same music folded into Trope: 'Half of the People', which opens with the text written by Paul Simon; and finally the nostalgic Trope: 'Thank You', for mezzo-soprano and instruments, based on classical idioms. 'VII. Meditation no. 2' is a modernist work for orchestra based on motives from Beethoven's Symphony no. 9 and somewhat reminiscent of Alban Berg, contrasted strongly by 'VIII. Epistle: The Word of the Lord', Bernstein's tribute to the music of Chilean *Nueva canción* composer Violeta Parra. The composer discovered the style, associated with left-wing politics, on one of his visits to South America, and with it Bernstein presented some of the most progressive politics heard in *Mass*. The 'IX. Gospel-sermon' for soloists, choir and instruments follows immediately with a wild mixture of marching band music and bluesy call-and-response, presenting an irreverent text. These latter two movements show how closely Bernstein's music can adhere to speech rhythms.

The next major section opens with 'X. Credo', which includes five contrasting subsections: 'Credo in unum Deum' for choir and orchestra, presented mechanically with disturbing percussion, mocking what is perhaps the rote nature of such creeds and returning in small segments throughout the larger section; Trope: 'Non credo', a confrontational solo with mocking choir that personalizes the believer's struggle; Trope: 'Hurry', a mixture between modernism, bluesy and folk sounds where a female soloist asks God to hurry his return; Trope: 'World Without End', a folk-based solo for another female soloist that continues the questioning mood; and Trope: 'I Believe in God', a solo for irreverent rock singer and appropriate instruments. The Celebrant's strident call for prayer finally leads to 'XI. Meditation no. 3' for choir and orchestra, which defiantly sets the text 'De profundis' (Psalm 131) in one of the work's most dramatic musical moments, including aleatoric climaxes where the choir shouts text in varied rhythms. 'De profundis, part 2' is the 'XII. Offertory', which combines material from 'Confiteor' and the chorale 'Almighty Father', finally leading to an instrumental version, heavy in the winds, of music heard earlier as 'In nomine patris'. Bernstein demonstrates the Celebrant's waning strength in 'XIII. The Lord's Prayer', the first movement of which is an introspective setting of the famous text, sung in a weak voice as the character also plays the melody on piano. The Celebrant then sings Trope: 'I Go On', a lonely number reminiscent of the opening of Symphony no. 2, 'The Age of Anxiety'. The number concludes with a bit of material from 'A Simple Song'.

'XIV. Sanctus' is a celebratory number for boys' choir and orchestra, followed by a solo for the Celebrant about a song that is about to fly from his very soul, his moment ending in a Hebrew text that is picked up by the choir as the Jewish Bernstein briefly foregrounds his own religion. Jack Gottlieb has written persuasively about the Jewish nature of *Mass*.[20] 'XV. Agnus Dei' follows without break, and it is here that any thoughts of peace are shattered by increasingly disruptive music. The texts 'dona nobis pacem' and 'miserere nobis' keep returning, upsetting the Celebrant, finally resulting in 'blues stanzas' where 'dona nobis pacem' is reduced

to a cynical ostinato over which soloists and chorus air doubts
and political protests. The Celebrant ends this section when he
shatters the Communion cup and plate and begins 'xvi. Fraction',
a fourteen-minute mad scene where Bernstein recapitulates many
motives from earlier in the show as the central character comes
completely unglued, doubting his faith in a number that touches
on many different moods. It is an extensive sequence, but *Mass* is
two hours long, and the Celebrant has been driven to this through
much of the work. He finally retires utterly broken and stripped
of his vestments. The work's conclusion then perhaps comes too
quickly, but there is dramatic power in the simplicity of 'xvii. Pax:
Communion'. It opens with material from the 'Epiphany' oboe solo,
followed by a boy recapitulating material from the end of 'A Simple
Song', suggesting that Bernstein's 'crisis of faith' might be resolved
by a child's naive faith. The tune gets passed to other members of
the cast and finally to the entire auditorium. The Celebrant returns,
refreshed and part of the communal celebration.

    Mass had one of the splashiest premieres in the history of
American music. The media found the combination of Bernstein's
huge work and the grand opening of Washington's performing arts
centre an irresistible draw, meaning that many critics weighed in
on the piece in newspapers, weekly news journals and the religious
and musical press. As Peter G. Davis noted, the work is 'a sitting
duck for the cynical'.[21] In the *New York Times*, Harold C. Schonberg
took his normal dim view of Bernstein's work, praising the 'skillful
lightweight music' that reminds one of Bernstein's Broadway works,
but finding the more serious moments 'pretentious and thin', and
damning Bernstein's lofty intentions: 'It is a showbiz Mass, the
work of a musician who desperately wants to be with it.'[22] Herman
Berlinski, a Jew writing in *Sacred Music*, published by the Roman
Catholic Church, provided a shrill condemnation from a variety
of angles, reflecting the Church's distress at seeing their sacred
texts used in a dramatic setting.[23] Noel Goemanne, writing in the

next issue of the same journal, dismisses Berlinski's comparison of Bernstein's work with mass settings of the past, noting that the composer never intended his work to be liturgical. He found the work's message useful because 'shocking as it may be, it is . . . a true picture of things happening in our churches these days.'[24] Reacting to the recording, Hugo Cole in the music journal *Tempo* praised Bernstein's sense of 'economy of musical means' and the score's rhythmic vitality, rating the popular idioms more successful than the composer's evocations of classical music. As time passes, Cole expected that the 'quality of musical invention' in *Mass* would become clearer.[25]

Mass has spoken to many over the years. Producer Roger Stevens reported that the audience greeted the conclusion of the premiere with three minutes of silence followed by thirty minutes of cheering.[26] The next summer the work had another run at the Kennedy Center, and in New York City impresario Sol Hurok put *Mass* on successfully at the Metropolitan Opera House for a month. By July 1972 the original cast recording had sold an astonishing 200,000 copies. Although difficult to mount, *Mass* has become a work that institutions produce when they wish to make a statement. It will never be Bernstein's most frequently performed piece, but it is one of his most revealing, personal works. The composer said in an interview that the work's musical 'surprises', brought on by the eclecticism, 'came from somewhere very deep' within him, and it was a work he had 'been writing all [his] life'.[27] Perhaps the most telling thing that he said in the interview, however, was his next comment: 'But in a way that's true of anybody's latest work, if it's a major one.'[28] The 'latest work', like *Mass*, was a major composition that just had to come out. The man had dug deep and birthed a magnum opus, something he simply needed to do. Seldom did Bernstein's well-honed sense of the dramatic get quite such a public airing.

The Harvard Lectures

Leonard Bernstein was 53 years old when *Mass* premiered.
Whatever else the piece might be, it was the most self-indulgent
composition of his career, and for the remainder of his life he also
seemed increasingly to prioritize his own desires and thoughts in
both his public projects and his private life.

While in Los Angeles for the new version of *Candide* and for
working on *Mass* with Stephen Schwartz, Bernstein met Tom
Cothran, director of music for a classical radio station. They began
a long relationship, with Cothran becoming an assistant accepted
by Bernstein's family, friends and associates, but he later came
between Bernstein and his wife. Among his duties for Bernstein
was serving as research assistant for the Norton Lectures, for
which he was on the Amberson payroll.

The Norton Lectures loomed, but in the year before going
to Cambridge in autumn 1972 Bernstein maintained his busy
conducting and filming schedule, including memorial projects
involving Stravinsky, who died in 1971, and filming works by
Mahler in Europe. Bernstein cancelled two operatic projects
in summer 1972, but honoured a contract to do *Carmen* at the
Metropolitan in New York in the autumn, a huge success both
in the production and as a recording. It was his first release with
Deutsche Grammophon, with whom he signed after finally leaving
CBS Records, where he no longer felt appreciated. The company,
worried about the bottom line, had insisted that Bernstein help
pay recording costs for *Mass*, but the album sold very well. As
a composer Bernstein was working on his ballet *Dybbuk* and
Broadway musical *1600 Pennsylvania Avenue*, described below.

His tenure as Charles Eliot Norton Professor of Poetry at
Harvard was for the 1972–3 academic year. This was one of
Bernstein's signature honours; previous recipients who were
composers included Stravinsky, Hindemith, Copland, Chávez

and Sessions. He was supposed to live at the college at various points during the two semesters, deliver six lectures and consult with students. He enjoyed his other duties so much – and was so busy with other projects – that he was unable to get the lectures finished for that academic year. Harvard allowed him to postpone the lectures until autumn 1973, and Bernstein made them into a multimedia extravaganza. His new manager Harry Kraut worked out the arrangements for the lectures to be published in book form, released as LP recordings and broadcast on public television, but Bernstein had to pay for the television production.[29] He filmed recorded examples with the Boston Symphony Orchestra to be shown during the lectures. Much of the work on the lectures was done by May 1973. He started to present them on 9 October at the largest available theatre (1,500 seats) in Cambridge, opening a six-week marathon in which he would rehearse each lecture once, present it to the live audience, and the next day record it for television. They were lengthy – the final one was four hours with an intermission – and he mostly memorized them but also had the text available on a teleprompter.

The Norton Lectures revealed much about Bernstein's musical interests and philosophy. He found his premise in applying Noam Chomsky's linguistic theories to such musical structures as chords, phrases, cadences and forms. The approach proved controversial, but few musical analyses find universal approbation among specialists. Bernstein anticipated by several years the importance of such an approach by music theorists. It remains compelling to explore Bernstein's many descriptions and analyses in the lectures, especially for twentieth-century music. For the serious musician Bernstein offered a useful model for unapologetic but approachable musical discussion, which musicians often allow to be compromised before a general audience. The lectures include telling looks at a number of compositions and remain provocative, if sometimes pretentious.

Beyond his association of linguistic models and music, Bernstein's Norton Lectures constitute his most serious defence of tonality in twentieth-century composition, a concern that also dominated his own creative output. For Bernstein, Stravinsky takes on a heroic status as a composer who remained modern and relevant while writing works that maintained a central pitch. Bernstein largely accepts the common notion of Schoenberg as Stravinsky's polar opposite and he sometimes travels a distance from more accepted analytical paths as he discredits Schoenberg's atonal efforts. Bernstein's obsession in contemporary music is ambiguity in almost every place that it might be found: melody, harmony, form, rhythm, metre and intervallic construction. In his quest for ambiguity, Bernstein painted a useful picture of the complexity of modern music.

Dybbuk

The next major creation in Bernstein's compositional life was his third and final ballet with Jerome Robbins, which he worked on primarily in 1973 and early 1974. Typically, the composer in him had to make space for many other activities. In a powerful statement against the Vietnam War that occurred at the same time as President Nixon's inaugural concert at the Kennedy Center in January 1973, Bernstein conducted Haydn's *Mass in Time of War* at the Washington Cathedral before an audience of 3,000, with thousands more listening outside the church. In late May and early June Bernstein took his entire family to Rome for an audience with Pope Paul vi, prior to conducting J. S. Bach's *Magnificat* and *Chichester Psalms* before the pontiff in a televised concert. Further activities that summer included attending a version of *Mass* in Vienna, conducted by his protégé John Mauceri; filming two Brahms symphonies for Unitel in Israel; and performing Mahler's

Symphony no. 2 at the Edinburgh Festival with the London Symphony Orchestra, and then filming that stirring version at Ely Cathedral near Cambridge. That summer he was too busy with the Norton Lectures and *Dybbuk* to teach at Tanglewood. In late November Bernstein attended a run-through with piano of Hal Prince's adaptation of *Candide*, which went on to a run of 740 performances on Broadway. Bernstein was not pleased with the removal of much of the score, but Prince's conception of the show in a circus-like atmosphere in a rebuilt theatre interior with action taking place in and around the audience brought *Candide* its longest run in New York.

The ballet *Dybbuk* is a potent reminder of Bernstein's Jewishness, and it forms one of his largest statements on his religious background. He had been considering collaborating with Robbins on the ballet since the 1940s.[30] Work in the 1970s proceeded slowly because the mercurial choreographer had great difficulty finalizing his conception. They based it on S. Ansky's Yiddish play *The Dybbuk*, which premiered in 1920 and profoundly moved Jewish audiences. It involved an impossible relationship between two young people promised to each other by their fathers before they were born. The boy dies and becomes a dybbuk, a spirit who occupies his love's soul. When she dies, their spirits unite in the afterlife. The play is full of Jewish mysticism and references to the Kabbalah, a discipline of esoteric teachings that Bernstein accessed to form some aspects of pitch organization in his score. He formed tone rows by converting symbols from the Kabbalah into numbers and relating them to various pitches. Besides obvious Jewish influences, Bernstein leaned heavily upon his knowledge of Stravinsky in the fifty-minute score, including the older composer's love for the octatonic scale, and he also set Hebrew texts sung by tenor and baritone soloists, *in toto* creating a fine example of his mature style. After the premiere Bernstein produced two orchestral suites, the first showcasing Jewish elements and sung portions and

The mature Bernstein in a characteristic conducting pose.

the second including more abstract music used in the ballet to depict the spiritual world. The composer premiered both suites in separate concerts with the New York Philharmonic in April 1975, but since then they have seldom been heard. The critical reaction to the ballet, originally entitled *Dybbuk Variations*, was positive, but the work never found public favour, even though Robbins reworked it twice, in 1975 and 1980.

In spring 1974 the Bernsteins moved to their final address, at the famous Dakota apartment building on Central Park West at 72nd Street, where John Lennon and Yoko Ono lived and outside which Lennon was assassinated in 1980. Nina was the only child left at home. Bernstein also bought a small apartment on the top floor to serve as his studio. Soon thereafter Felicia had a breast cancer scare that only family and friends knew about; after a mastectomy she recovered, but it was a temporary respite.[31] Despite his own brief hospitalization for shortness of breath in summer 1974, Bernstein resumed his frenetic activities, teaching and conducting at Tanglewood and leading the New York Philharmonic in Mahler's Symphony no. 5 in Central Park before an audience of 100,000 people, before leaving with the orchestra on a tour of New Zealand, Australia and Japan, splitting the conducting duties with Philharmonic director Pierre Boulez. Through 1975 he balanced his work on *1600 Pennsylvania Avenue* with Alan Jay Lerner with conducting in New York and Europe. A highlight of the year was a filmed concert of Berlioz's titanic *Requiem* at the famous Church of Les Invalides in Paris with a bevy of Parisian musicians.

1600 Pennsylvania Avenue

The Broadway business is brutal. Most shows fail, and what one has accomplished in the past guarantees nothing on future efforts.

One might expect that a show with a score by the composer of *West Side Story* and lyrics and book by the author of *My Fair Lady* would have an excellent chance for success, but on the way to the premiere the show's tone became too preachy and the story too convoluted. Bernstein returned to New York in September 1975 to finish the show, but producer Arnold Saint-Subber had left the project because of what appeared to be insoluble problems with Lerner's book. Bernstein's friend Roger Stevens and Robert Whitehead stepped into the breach, but were unwilling to proceed without a workable book.[32] Lerner 'saved' the project by inducing the Coca-Cola Company to invest most of the required money, with the contract mandating a Broadway opening. The writer, therefore, could not be forced to fix the book through threat of cancellation.

The premise of *1600 Pennsylvania Avenue* was to have the same four actors portray multiple presidents, first ladies and slaves/servants throughout American history. It was an unwieldy and complicated conception by liberal authors lecturing their fellow citizens on race problems in the United States – perhaps not a bad idea, but certainly not what audiences wanted to hear in the spring of 1976 when preparing for the American Bicentennial. At one point Bernstein asked Robbins to come see the show and perhaps help with it, but his frequent collaborator said that it could not be fixed. There were many problems during rehearsals and in out-of-town try-outs. *1600 Pennsylvania Avenue* opened to disastrous reviews on 8 May 1976 and closed after seven performances. Burton calls the show Bernstein's 'worst failure of his professional life'.[33] He was so disappointed that he refused to allow a recording of his score. He went on holiday to Mexico with Felicia to lick his wounds.

The show did not work, but it included moments of brilliance from both Bernstein and Lerner, as may be appreciated in *The White House Cantata*, released in 1997 by the Bernstein Estate in an attempt to make most of the score available in concert form. A recording, issued three years later, emphasizes the work's operatic possibilities with singers Thomas Hampson and June Anderson and the London Symphony Orchestra directed by Kent Nagano.[34] The disc demonstrates that Humphrey Burton was too harsh when he stated that in *1600 Pennsylvania Avenue* the composer 'was only intermittently working at the highest level of invention and he was surprisingly self-indulgent'.[35] There are many moments in the score when both Bernstein and Lerner were wonderfully creative, with witty lyrics that describe character and dramatic situations and music that emanates from all parts of the composer's eclectic inspirations, often with intelligent parody of patriotic tropes that Bernstein uses both seriously and ironically. The one song that became known outside of the show was the anthem-like 'Take Care of this House', one of Bernstein's most lyrical conceptions, celebrating the best of American, democratic intentions. In the show the first lady sings it to the African American son of the servants, eloquent recognition that members of each race are part of the United States, both with hopes and dreams. The opening musical sequence, 'Ten Square Miles by the Potomac River', includes clever lyrics and delightful music in service of dramatizing the compromise that, among other things, caused the nation's capital to be carved out of Virginia and Maryland. Bernstein uses moments of dense counterpoint to approximate truncated political debate and provides ebullient music for Lerner's cheeky, knowing lyrics that wink at American history. The composer of the parodies of various types of music in *Candide* comes alive in the chorus 'The Grand Old Party', another number with effective lyrics, and 'Duet for One' is a brilliant musico-theatrical moment sung by the same actress playing two first ladies. The debacle that was *1600 Pennsylvania Avenue* left a major, and sometimes brilliant, score by Bernstein in the shadows.

Songfest

An interesting outline of Leonard Bernstein, the man and musician, emerges in *Songfest*, which partly came out of his relationship with Tom Cothran.[36] This was Bernstein's Bicentennial concert work, bringing together poems by American writers from the seventeenth to the twentieth century in a song cycle for six different singers and large orchestra. Bernstein and Cothran read poems together and chose them jointly. A number of movements seem to represent Bernstein's life at the time and the work is a major musical success, but the large number of soloists and Bernstein's expansive use of orchestra has severely limited the number of times that the piece has been heard. The premiere of the full set took place with the composer conducting the National Symphony in Washington, DC, on 11 October 1977.

Songfest is a fine reminder of Bernstein's gift for writing for voices, and the orchestra effectively supports his interpretation of the poems. He again accesses a heady mixture of musical styles, stitching together an impressive musical quilt that includes thirteen poems placed in twelve movements for various numbers of singers. Works by some of America's best-known poets appear. Bernstein and Cothran made selections that highlighted the 'Others' in American society, especially homosexuals, African Americans and Latinas, a cornucopia of outcasts from 1970s America being celebrated for the Bicentennial. 'To the Poem' by Frank O'Hara opens the set with mock seriousness about doing 'something grand', which Bernstein approached with cheeky grandiloquence. Lawrence Ferlinghetti's 'The Pennycandystore Beyond the El', a memory of a young man's sexual awakening, is set to an eerie twelve-tone row and swing rhythms. 'A Julia de Burgos', a text named after the Puerto Rican poet, is a feminist text in Spanish with a setting that charges forward with unpredictable rhythms. 'To What You Said . . .' is by Walt Whitman, unpublished in his lifetime, in which he admitted his own homosexuality and comments on his awkward fit in society, a revealing text for Bernstein to use at this moment in his life and a song of special beauty. His concern for African Americans appears in a jaunty treatment of two poems, 'I, Too, Sing America' by Langston Hughes and 'Okay "Negroes"' by June Jordan. 'To My Dear and Loving Husband' is by seventeenth-century poet Anne Bradstreet, crafted here memorably for a trio of women, a strong endorsement of marriage composed when Bernstein was in crisis with his own. 'Storyette H. M.' by Gertrude Stein concerns a couple, one going out and enjoying it, and the other staying home unhappily. The topic is so close to the situation between Bernstein and his wife at that moment that the choice seems almost cruel, and the composer set it energetically, perhaps unsparingly. The poem 'if you can't eat you got to' by e e cummings concerns thoughtful, bohemian artists, provided with music that approaches swing rhythms sung by popular vocal groups. Conrad Aiken's 'Music That I Heard With You' is a memory of lost love, set beautifully in a mixture of diatonic and twelve-tone writing. 'Zizi's Lament', a poem by Gregory Corso, is a sardonic look at a North African entertainer. Bernstein accesses Middle Eastern tropes for this bitter text, perhaps evoking another American minority. Edna St Vincent Millay's 'What Lips My Lips Have Kissed' drew serious treatment from Bernstein that includes some of his most interesting speech rhythms. The finale is 'Israfel', with text by Edgar Allan Poe, an unusual choice with a title referencing the Islamic angel who will blow the trumpet at the end of time; Poe praises the angel and comments on his own verses. Bernstein takes his cue from the poet and wrote a virtuosic setting for singers and orchestra, at times interrupting the movement with percussion and obnoxious chords.

A Sad End

While working on *1600 Pennsylvania Avenue* and pursuing such
conducting opportunities as leading the New York Philharmonic on
tours in honour of the American Bicentennial, Bernstein's marriage
unravelled. The informal arrangement that the couple had worked
out – with Bernstein pursuing relationships with men that Felicia
did not want to know about – had worked, probably with difficult
moments, for over two decades. In the 1970s, however, American
society was very different from how it had been in the early 1950s
when they married. Homosexuality was still not accepted by a large
percentage of the American public, but many more homosexuals
had come out of the closet since the Stonewall riots in New York
City in 1969. Surely Bernstein noticed that it was easier now to live
as an openly gay man, and he clearly was considering the possibility.
A public indication came at a performance of Shostakovich's
Symphony no. 14 with the New York Philharmonic in December
1976, after he had separated from Felicia. The 58-year-old conductor
spoke to the audience for fifteen minutes before performing the
piece, comparing himself with the composer, who was 63 when he
wrote the symphony. Bernstein said that 'as death approaches' a
composer must find 'complete freedom', which he intended to do.[37]
While not a public confession of his homosexuality, it was a striking
moment of honesty when Bernstein wrestled between what seems
to have been the dominant part of his true sexuality and his feelings
for his wife and the mother of his three children.

Bernstein was in love with Tom Cothran and wanted to live
with him. He left an angry, frustrated Felicia and went to California
with his lover in August and September 1976, the move to another
coast suggested by his manager Harry Kraut, trying to take the
hometown press out of the situation.[38] In the middle of September
they returned to New York and lived at a hotel, with Bernstein
continuing his conducting in the United States and Europe

The Dakota Apartments on Central Park West at 72nd Street, where Bernstein and his family moved in 1974, and where he died in 1990.

(travelling with Cothran) and also seeing his family. The press discovered the fractured marriage in late October. In January 1977 Bernstein and Cothran went to Palm Springs for the winter, but the next month Bernstein returned to New York and told Kraut that he could not live with Cothran and wanted to reconcile with Felicia. Bernstein and Cothran proved ill-suited to each other domestically. The musician and his wife started to be seen together in public, but he also still spent time with Cothran, such as ten days in Morocco in late winter. Newspapers reported in mid-June that Bernstein was back with Felicia, and they were to leave soon for a month in Austria, where the town of Villach was having a Bernstein Festival, and then he would lead the Israel Philharmonic on a German tour. Felicia, however, was diagnosed with lung cancer, and sent her husband to Austria without telling him, promising to come soon. Bernstein finally learned the truth and flew home, where he found her the best care possible. Radiation treatments and extensive chemotherapy did not cure Felicia, who lived in pain for almost two years, dying on 16 June 1978, long after doctors had given up on her future. Despite the fact that Felicia had been a lifelong smoker, the grieving Bernstein blamed himself for her death, perhaps because her diagnosis came so soon after their separation.

Sexuality was a powerful force in this complex man. He was unable to remain loyal to Felicia in a traditional manner, but she had always been a sort of anchor, providing the home and family that Bernstein craved, and perhaps also giving him the front that he needed to pursue his career. His homosexuality was difficult for him. Letters from the 1940s show a man seeking a 'cure' – considered possible by psychologists at the time – and when I interviewed the man in 1982 he was curious about this young student writing a thesis on Copland's influence on him. He said that he would not ask me if I had 'a problem with homosexuality', but then spoke of the 'agony' of the condition.[39] Although it is not acceptable today to speak this way about homosexuality, Bernstein was born in 1918 and, despite his lifelong liberal leanings, he remained a creature of his generation; 'nice Jewish boys' did not have these feelings. In a bit more than an hour with Leonard Bernstein, I hardly got to know him, but the man seemingly spoke his mind to everyone. At another moment he found out I was to be married soon, and he smiled broadly and expressed his strong approval of being wed. Felicia Bernstein perhaps allowed Bernstein to be the person that Koussevitzky, and maybe his own father, wanted him to be: husband, father, pillar of the community. Without her, his world spiralled dangerously out of control, and he seemed to do little to try and prolong his own life. Certainly flashes of brilliance remained, but the final chapter of Bernstein's life is often a sad journey.

7

'And all the spooks of swift-advancing age': Music at the Close, 1978–90

Just after Felicia's death, Bernstein sought solace with his two siblings and went for a cruise off Greece on the Unitel corporate yacht.[1] The end of the summer included a celebration of his sixtieth birthday hosted by the National Symphony Orchestra at Wolf Trap, outside Washington, DC, an event that Bernstein felt obligated to attend because it was a fundraiser for the cash-strapped ensemble. It was broadcast live on PBS, and this author as a young musician loved every moment of it, but Bernstein surely had to put on a brave face for it.

The emotional toll of Felicia's death complicated Bernstein's pursuit of his many projects, but, paradoxically, her untimely passing also left him with freedom to live his life as he pleased. His parenting responsibilities were not over, with Nina aged sixteen when her mother died, but Jamie and Alexander were in their early to mid-twenties. Bernstein had fruitful relationships with several orchestras that included the expectation of regular collaborations, but he was not nearly as involved with any one group as he had been with the New York Philharmonic as music director. He tried to have the freedom to compose several months each year, and during the remainder of his life he finished several major works and a number of minor ones, but his writing remained sporadic and dependent upon his conducting schedule. It seems to be how Bernstein functioned best, perhaps satisfying his debt to Koussevitzky by conducting, allowing him to make memorable music with a variety of orchestras. In this chapter we will first consider this aspect of his late career, including his general tendencies in travelling and working, and several highlights of his work.

The Conductor who Lived at Thirty Thousand Feet

Bernstein began his life as a guest conductor in the 1940s travelling by train and ship, but his performing life in the late 1970s was unthinkable without the modern jet. He lived in New York and Connecticut, usually conducted for longer periods in Europe than his own country, and continued to work in Israel and increasingly in Asia, primarily with Western orchestras on tour. He worked consistently with the Vienna Philharmonic, including in twelve of the last thirteen years of his life. He performed with the New York Philharmonic and Boston Symphony Orchestra each during nine of those years, the Israel Philharmonic and Bavarian Radio Symphony Orchestra each for eight, and the National Symphony in Washington during seven of those years. Between 1983 and 1990 he worked with the Santa Cecilia Orchestra in Rome during five of those years, and he conducted the London Philharmonic in each of the last three years of his life.[2] Bernstein travelled with a staff of three – his manager Harry Kraut, a personal assistant and a conducting assistant – and often a travelling companion, a friend (like Betty Comden) or his current male paramour. Bernstein's visit to a city often included parties and meetings with heads of state and other prominent people, and he stayed in favourite suites in hotels with great views. His personal assistant would go on ahead to make sure that all was set at the next hotel. The conductor did not necessarily expect the orchestra to foot the bill for this luxury, often paying for the suites himself, and ensembles with which he worked regularly did not pay his full fee.[3]

Bernstein was a wealthy man who perhaps did not need the income that he made as a guest conductor, but he clearly needed the stimulus of working with first-class orchestras and the resultant adulation. The music-making and occasions had to have been memorable, because such orchestras would not have countenanced a demanding maestro who did not deliver the goods. In March 1982 I observed a rehearsal with the National Symphony where Bernstein felt that he needed overtime to finish preparations for the concert, and more than once he complained loudly. The general manager finally granted his wish and the maestro made good use of the extra rehearsal.

One could fill an entire volume chronicling Bernstein's late peregrinations as a guest conductor, and the story would quickly become repetitious, but there were a number of special events or seasons that were remarkable. Three months after his wife's death he dived back into conducting, going to Vienna where he directed and filmed five Beethoven symphonies for Unitel (part of what became a complete set) and then did *Songfest* in Munich. His 1979 European work late in the year included Bernstein's unprecedented appearance with the Berlin Philharmonic – Herbert von Karajan's orchestra – in two performances of Mahler's Symphony no. 9, a benefit for Amnesty International, one of Bernstein's favourite causes. Burton reports that he had a few problems bringing the orchestra around to his emotional style of conducting, but the interpretation became a fine recording.[4] In October 1979 the Vienna Philharmonic came to Washington's Kennedy Center for a three-week season, performances that Bernstein shared with Zubin Mehta and Karl Böhm. Bernstein led two concerts and five performances of *Fidelio*, and then a concert version of the opera with the orchestra in Avery Fisher Hall in New York. From the end of 1979, Bernstein disappeared from the podium for thirteen months to work on composition projects.

Despite announcing that he had found an operatic project – the work that became *A Quiet Place* – Bernstein spent six months conducting in 1981, including conducting his 'Kaddish' at the Vatican with Pope John Paul II, who was recovering from an assassination attempt, listening on a closed circuit feed in his room. The conductor considered his major project in 1981 to be his recording of Wagner's *Tristan and Isolde* with the Bavarian Radio Symphony Orchestra in Munich.[5] Bernstein had loved the opera throughout his career, certainly an acquired taste for a Jewish conductor given Wagner's well-documented anti-Semitism. The project was mammoth, involving live, concert performances of each of the three acts separately in January, April and November with recordings made live and material captured in rehearsals used as needed. Bernstein followed his own muse, favouring slower tempos as heard in nineteenth-century performances. The results generated varied critical responses, but it was a stunning reading of the work that he was proud to have completed, stating: 'My life is complete. I don't care what happens after this. It is the finest thing I've ever done.'[6] He also ran into headwinds concerning deliberate tempos in spring 1982 when he led the BBC Symphony Orchestra in a performance of his *Songfest* and Edward Elgar's *Enigma Variations*. The tempo at which he took the latter work struck British musicians as extraordinarily slow and Burton reports that the performance was about ten minutes longer than was customary for the piece.[7] On the Deutsche Grammophon recording, however, Bernstein's timing is 29:23, very close to traditional thinking on the work.[8] As musicians are aware, unmeasured perception of tempo is at best subjective. A major focus for Bernstein for the remainder of spring 1982 was performing works by Stravinsky in the centenary year of his birth in a tour with the Israel Philharmonic in West Germany, Mexico and Texas, and additional performances of the composer's works in Milan, Venice and Washington. In a brief period of estrangement from the Boston Symphony Orchestra and Tanglewood, Bernstein spearheaded the formation of a training institute for young musicians in association with the Los Angeles Philharmonic, where he taught in summer 1982.

A telling document concerning Bernstein the conductor is a video of recording sessions of *West Side Story* for Deutsche Grammophon, made in 1984 with a hand-picked orchestra and mostly operatic singers.[9] The project was problematic from the beginning – the show's music is not operatic, and the likes of Kiri Te Kanawa is not the sound one associates with the role of Maria – but Bernstein clearly gloried in hearing his music sung by fine voices with a fuller orchestra than one hears from a theatre pit. Bernstein's hand is all over the video, including clips of interviews with him and voiceovers in the film. He allowed artistic bumps in the road with fellow performers and sound engineers, usually behind the scenes, to appear in the film, which presents a number of sides of Bernstein's musical and performance personalities. It is a compelling document that is perhaps more interesting than the recording that resulted from the sessions, where Jose Carreras as Tony was unable to disguise his heavy Spanish accent and the composer at times adopted mannered, slow tempos. Whatever the faults, Joan Peyser noted a few years after the recording appeared that at the time it was Deutsche Grammophon's best-selling album ever.[10] The video of the recording sessions is one of several that Bernstein made or started in the 1980s, a continuation of his educational activities.

Bernstein combined his status as an international conductor and celebrity with one of his more profound political statements in August 1985, the fortieth anniversary of the atomic bombing of Hiroshima and Nagasaki. He led his 'Kaddish' in two performances in Hiroshima with soprano Barbara Hendricks, a Viennese youth choir and the European Community Youth Orchestra, performances that also included Japanese conductor Eiji Oue (a Bernstein mentee from Tanglewood) leading two other works. One of Bernstein's major causes was nuclear disarmament, and he had enough to say concerning the subject that the American Embassy announced that the conductor was in Hiroshima on a personal mission, without official status. The conductor's schedule in the weeks following Hiroshima almost defied reason: an immediate return to Europe with the orchestra for concerts in Budapest and Vienna, off to Germany to help establish a new orchestral festival in Schleswig-Holstein, and then to Tel Aviv to join the Israel Philharmonic for a tour to Munich and yet another visit to Japan. Bernstein had nothing to prove at this point in his career, but he remained fanatically driven as a conductor.

Bernstein's ability to make a huge splash while making music continued unabated to the end of his life, even in the last year when his health was failing him. The year 1986 included recording his opera *A Quiet Place* in a live performance in Vienna with the Vienna State Opera. He conducted a concert, including his *Chichester Psalms, Serenade* and 'The Age of Anxiety', at London's Barbican Centre in May during a two-week Bernstein Festival. Queen Elizabeth II attended the performance. In 1987 he conducted Mahler's first five symphonies in seven months with the Amsterdam Concertgebouw, New York Philharmonic and Vienna Philharmonic, in addition to leading the latter ensemble at the prestigious Salzburg Festival. In August 1988 Tanglewood hosted a huge celebration of Bernstein's seventieth birthday, where he conducted among a long list of other famed musicians. On 1 September 1989 he took part in a concert in Warsaw coinciding with the fiftieth anniversary of the start of the Second World War, leading Beethoven's *Leonore* Overture no. 3 and *Chichester Psalms* in a performance that included a number of classical music luminaries and was broadcast in Europe, the United States and Japan. Later in the autumn he was in Bonn leading performances for a three-week festival dedicated to his works and those of their native son Beethoven, followed by returning to New York for all-Copland and all-Tchaikovsky performances with the Philharmonic. In December he was in London for a concert version and recording of *Candide*, a project that worked better than the realization of *West Side Story* five years before. Bernstein and his organization then managed to make him a central figure in the celebration of the dismantling of the Berlin Wall with a televised and recorded performance of Beethoven's Symphony no. 9 in the Schauspielhaus in East Berlin on Christmas Day. Performers included the Bavarian Radio Symphony Orchestra and Chorus and members of orchestras from Dresden, Leningrad, London, New York and Paris. The project's realization was assisted by Bernstein's increased performance presence in Berlin in the late 1980s, but it was utterly remarkable that an American Jewish conductor became celebrator-in-chief for a German event of such world significance.

Burton describes a scary moment on 23 December, when Bernstein seemed to lose consciousness after reaching complete exhaustion following *two* preliminary performances of Beethoven's Ninth in both East and West Berlin.[11] It was perhaps an early indication of the cancer and other illnesses that would kill him less than ten months later. Through 1990, however, during the rapid decline of his health, his conducting activities included three concerts with the Vienna Philharmonic at Carnegie Hall and Mozart's Mass in C minor in a televised concert with the Bavarian Radio Symphony Orchestra and Chorus in the winter, Beethoven's Ninth to close the Prague Spring Festival, a busy trip to Japan in the summer for the new Pacific Music Festival (a Tanglewood-like event that Bernstein helped found) from which he came home early in a state of collapse, and a final visit to Tanglewood in August where he taught and conducted. He led Beethoven's Symphony no. 7 in the Koussevitzky Memorial Concert on 19 August, during which he had a horrible coughing fit during the third movement, but he gamely finished the performance.[12] Not long before his death on 14 October 1990, Bernstein's organization announced his retirement from conducting, alerting the musical world that he was deathly ill.

Late Compositions

Bernstein completed eight major works after his wife's death. He started or considered a number of others, but writing music became more difficult for him as he aged, and there was always more conducting to do. Several of his late works show a probing musical mind at work solving compositional problems, but only one has truly made its way into the repertory: the song cycle *Arias and Barcarolles*. As will be shown below, several of these other pieces are significant entries in his catalogue, but they remain lesser known than Bernstein's earlier works in the same genres. A possible reason for this is that the most significant conductor of Bernstein's works during his lifetime was the composer himself, which especially helped his orchestral pieces to become known. Bernstein, who died at the relatively young age of 72, simply had less time to help his late works to enter the repertory.

The Boston Symphony Orchestra commissioned Bernstein to write something for their centenary season, and mostly in August 1980 he produced his Divertimento for Orchestra, a light-hearted look at growing up as a musician in Boston. He linked the movements with the notes 'B' and 'C' (for 'Boston Centennial') and the resulting intervals. According to Jack Gottlieb's programme note, Bernstein originally intended what became the opening 'Sennets and Tuckets' movement to be the entire composition, but his manipulations of the two notes produced more ideas than he expected and caused him to write eight short movements that are about fifteen minutes total.[13] Following the opening, the Divertimento includes 'Waltz', 'Mazurka', 'Samba', 'Turkey Trot', 'Sphinxes', 'Blues' and 'In Memoriam; March: "The BSO Forever"'. Material from 'Sennets and Tuckets' reappears in later movements, especially the closing march, and several sections of the work would be comfortable in *Candide*, another place where Bernstein wrote versions of various dances. The 'Waltz' is especially charming, sounding a great deal like the type in triple metre despite its 7/8 time signature. With short movements, quotations of standard repertory in honour of concerts that he heard as a boy and segments with tongue thrust firmly in cheek, Bernstein brought little gravitas to the Divertimento.

Bernstein composed *Halil, Nocturne* in memory of Yadin Tenenbaum, a nineteen-year-old Israeli flautist who met his untimely end in the 1973 Arab-Israeli War. (*Halil* is Hebrew for 'flute'.) Bernstein never met Tenenbaum, but in his programme note he stated, 'I know his spirit.'[14] He wrote the piece in winter 1980–81, basing some of it on *CBS Music*, a score from 1977 that he had withdrawn. Scored for solo flute, piccolo and alto flute (the latter two 'must sound from a distance and be unseen'), an extensive percussion section (five players), harp and strings, *Halil* is another work where Bernstein veers between tonality and atonality, opening with twelve-tone writing and moving to a lyrical, tonal melody that could sound in any number of his works.[15] The composer labelled the piece 'an ongoing conflict of nocturnal images', and it concludes tranquilly.[16] Bernstein premiered the piece with flautist Jean-Pierre Rampal and the Israel Philharmonic on 27 May 1981 and conducted it several more times in the next few years. It is very attractive but has failed to become well known. Bernstein also prepared a version for flute, piano and percussion.

The Van Cliburn International Piano Competition has a history of commissioning test pieces. Bernstein supplied the work for the sixth competition in 1981. *Touches: Chorale, Eight Variations and Coda* appears to be the composer's tribute to his beloved Piano Variations by Copland. Both works are variation sets that flow easily from one section to another with each variation based on material that has preceded it. Like Copland's piece, *Touches* also included references to jazz and blues, but in the Bernstein the tropes from these styles are more part of the foreground. *Touches* is a carefully conceived work that has been approached by a number of pianists and a fine example of Bernstein's mature, serious music.

Bernstein longed to write a memorable opera. One can hardly fault him for not fulfilling this lofty ambition, but he certainly tried. *Trouble in Tahiti* met mixed reviews and was too short to be the 'Great American Opera', but the composer felt strongly enough about its theme and characters to revisit the family in *A Quiet Place*, jointly commissioned by the Houston Grand Opera, Washington National Opera and Milan's Teatro alla Scala. For his librettist, Bernstein found Stephen Wadsworth, who was about thirty years old at the time of their collaboration. They bonded over losses in their families – Bernstein was still mourning Felicia, and Wadsworth's sister had recently died – and together wrote a work where the declamation mimicked how Americans talk.[17] Bernstein had always been interested in applying speech rhythms to his vocal music, but he never went further with the possibility than in *A Quiet Place*, where many rhythms in vocal lines seem unnecessarily complicated until one realizes how closely normal speech patterns have been approximated. In reviewing the original version, Andrew Porter of the *New Yorker* stated: 'The melodic lines are as sharp-eared as Janáček's in their transformations of speech rhythms and speech inflections into music.'[18] The opening finds Sam at his wife Dinah's funeral; she has died in an apparently drunken car accident. Also attending are Junior, the couple's psychotic son, and their daughter Dede, whose husband François used to be Junior's lover. Together they take care of Junior. The opera's theme involves a troubled family trying to communicate, which they haltingly do by the close. It is a blunt story based on unpleasant situations, with some, as in *Trouble in Tahiti*, that seem perilously close to Bernstein's own life. Some audience members might find the view too close to contemporary reality, unlike many operas where distant tragedies may be experienced cathartically. One must wonder at this point if the opera will ever enter the repertory. Bernstein and

Wadsworth used *Trouble in Tahiti* as a flashback, and its placement in the larger opera was a major part of revisions that took place after the Washington, DC, premiere and before performances in Houston and Milan. Conductor John Mauceri, a Bernstein protégé, suggested a new order for the flashbacks and new material, which many considered an improvement. Bernstein's musical style is different in *A Quiet Place* when compared to *Trouble in Tahiti*, not surprisingly for material composed three decades apart, but this problem is mitigated by the fact that flashbacks sound like an earlier period. Although fonder of the first version, Porter wrote the following about the revised version: 'It's a bold, ambitious, and very interesting opera, containing some of Bernstein's most richly wrought music.'[19] Porter's evaluation was more positive than that of many reviewers, but listeners who desire a profound knowledge of Bernstein's music must get to know *A Quiet Place*.

The general lack of knowledge concerning Bernstein's later orchestral works certainly applies to his *Concerto for Orchestra*, composed over a three-year period. Two movements premiered as *Jubilee Games* in 1986, a response to a commission from the Israel Philharmonic. At the premiere, the composer announced that he would add more to it, which he did in stages, finally resulting in 1989 in four movements: 'Free-style Events', 'Mixed Doubles (Theme and Seven Variations)', 'Diaspora Dances' and 'Benediction'. The opening includes orchestral improvisation, unusual for Bernstein, and prerecorded tapes, resulting in some stridently dissonant structures. 'Mixed Doubles' is a tribute to the second movement of Béla Bartók's *Concerto for Orchestra*, called 'Play of the Couples'. Based upon Variations on an Octatonic Scale that Bernstein composed in 1988–9, 'Mixed Doubles' includes an emphasis on chamber music textures. Bernstein's third movement, 'Diaspora Dances', somewhat reminiscent of Bartók's dance music, is a catchy Vivace, while the finale is a setting of a peaceful text from Numbers 6:24–6 with a baritone singing the verses in Hebrew. The vocal portion encompasses only the last two minutes, so short that the composer allows that it could be prerecorded. The 'Benediction' is a thoughtful closing to a career that had resulted in several works based upon Hebrew texts.

When working on the *Concerto for Orchestra*, Bernstein also adapted his incidental score for *The Lark* (1955) into a *Missa brevis* after a commission from Robert Shaw, who premiered the piece with the Atlanta Symphony Orchestra and Chorus in 1988. The score includes far more influence from medieval and Renaissance music than one usually hears from Bernstein, but it is recognizably his and should be a delightful discovery for those interested in lesser-known corners of his oeuvre.

Arias and Barcarolles (1988) is perhaps the best of Bernstein's late works, a bracing song cycle exploring aspects of love that is moving, funny and varied. The enigmatic title derives from a comment that President Eisenhower made after Bernstein played Gershwin's *Rhapsody in Blue* at the White House with the New York Philharmonic in 1960. Comparing the composition to more classical selections also on the programme, Eisenhower said, 'I like music with a theme, not all them [*sic*] arias and barcarolles.'[20] Bernstein wrote the cycle in April 1988 for an AIDS fundraising performance. The final version is eight songs for mezzo-soprano, baritone and piano played four-hands. Bernstein wrote the lyrics, except for 'Little Smary', a bedtime story his mother told him as a child, and '*Oif Mayn Khas'neh*' by Yiddish poet Yankev-Yitskhok Segal. 'Prelude', based upon a song that Bernstein wrote for his daughter Jamie's wedding, includes singers intoning thoughts of love over an angry piano part, introducing the cycle's ambiguous mood. 'Love Duet' is a consideration of mundane questions in married life along with clever commentary on the song's music, while 'Little Smary' (for mezzo) chronicles a child's angst while listening to a vivid story. 'The Love of My Life' (for baritone) features a man wondering if his love will arrive, or if the person might have already come, a fascinating contrast with 'Greeting' (for mezzo), an innocent song that Bernstein wrote after his son Alexander was born. The baritone sings the Yiddish song about a klezmer musician who turns a wedding upside down, followed by 'Mr and Mrs Webb Say Goodnight', a humorous look at marital pillow talk inspired by the family of Dean Charles Webb of the Indiana University School of Music, whom Bernstein got to know while in residence there in the winter of 1982. The final movement, 'Nachspiel', is for pianists with both singers humming, a lovely song that Bernstein wrote in 1986 for his mother's birthday.

The final completed work of Bernstein's career was the *Dance Suite* for brass quintet, five movements composed for the fiftieth anniversary gala of the American Ballet Theater on 14 January 1990. Intended as music for dance, the choreographer decided the movements were of insufficient length. At the gala the Empire Brass performed the suite.

Although these are the only late works that Bernstein completed, he explored ideas for a number of other pieces and wrote music for some of them. Humphrey Burton describes about half a dozen such projects from the time of his wife's death to Bernstein's own demise, and notes in more than one instance that the problem was the composer's obsession with writing a significant work, a serious, perhaps great piece that could form a substantive part of his legacy, certainly not the way to compose something spontaneous. Soon after Felicia died, Bernstein corresponded with Tom Cothran about a possible opera of the novel *Lolita*, but they could not decide how the young title character might be realized in operatic terms.[21] At the start of his year-long 'sabbatical' to compose in December 1979, Bernstein began a possible musical film on the auto industry pioneer Preston Tucker with lyricists Comden and Green and director Francis Ford Coppola, but the latter figure lost interest after little work had been done.[22] Bernstein progressed further with Arthur Laurents on a possible opera or musical theatre piece

entitled *Alarums and Flourishes*, but Nina Bernstein convinced her
father that the story was too close to *Pippin*, ending a project that
consumed about six months of his year off from conducting.[23]
Concern for writing a memorable work seemed to be a major
problem with a possible opera involving the Holocaust for which
a plot never emerged with Stephen Wadsworth in 1984–5, and
Bernstein continued working on the piece under the title *Babel*
with another collaborator, John Wells, into the last year of his
life.[24] That same year, Jerome Robbins re-interested Bernstein
in an adaptation of Bertolt Brecht's *The Exception and the Rule*,
which they had previously approached with Stephen Sondheim in
summer 1968.[25] This time the composer worked for three months
with playwright John Guare. Working under the title *The Race to
Urga*, the team reached the stage of open rehearsals, but Burton
quotes a memorandum that Bernstein sent to his collaborators
that they must take their work and 'justify our efforts morally; we
are ethically bound to reach an affluent public at all costs and by
all means'. The work apparently failed to meet this high standard
and was stillborn.[26] There is an element of tragedy in seeing a gifted
composer doom works late in his career by placing unrealistic
expectations on the results.

Personal Matters

It does not appear to have been simple to be Leonard Bernstein or
to be closely associated with him in the last twelve years of his life.
His conducting career hummed along in high gear, but apparently
he composed successfully only when he was able to shed crippling
expectations. His family remained an important part of his life, as
seen, for example, in the close relationship that developed between
him and his younger daughter, Nina, while she was still at home.
The older daughter, Jamie, married David Thomas in 1984. He was

a calm man who perhaps helped stabilize his father-in-law, and soon grandchildren appeared – but Bernstein's eldest daughter has spoken bluntly about the later years: 'After my mother was gone . . . there was no one to check him except us and there were limits for us because we didn't live with him. So after that it was just Maestro City all the way.'[27] It was a close family and there were light moments, but Jamie noted that Bernstein's frequent mixture of Scotch and Dexedrine (an amphetamine) contributed to his inconsistent behaviour, unlike the sweet father that she had always known. Bernstein had never been abstemious when it came to alcohol and he was no stranger to seeking assistance from various prescription drugs, but there were a number of signs that these habits got out of hand later in his life.

Bernstein and Tom Cothran remained friends after Felicia's death, even as Bernstein's amorous interests moved on to other men. Burton treats at some length letters that Cothran wrote to Bernstein in his first few years as a widower with solid advice concerning his life and work, urging him, for example, to go back to writing musical comedies and to conduct less so that he would have more time for composition. It almost seems that Cothran might have become a valuable counsellor, but he was diagnosed with lymphoma in 1980, and soon after that with AIDS. A visit to his bedside in November 1986 inspired Bernstein to work with manager Harry Kraut on fundraising for AIDS research, soon thereafter, in association with other artists, collecting $300,000 in a concert at the Public Theater, and the next year $1.7 million in a performance at Carnegie Hall. AIDS, along with Amnesty International, the Save the Children Fund, racial harmony and various peace and nuclear disarmament, formed the causes that the socially conscious Bernstein advocated in his last decade.

Bernstein's powerful libido was no less important to him after his wife died, and from that point he primarily appears to have sought relationships with men. There were a number of passionate attachments, mostly partners much younger than Bernstein and a number of them musicians. Burton provides descriptions from some of Bernstein's lovers involving ties formed through mutual interests in puzzles or poetry, and the single-mindedness that he brought to such liaisons.[28] Several of these men became intimate friends with Bernstein and remained in his orbit after the passion had cooled, but things could become messy when Bernstein became interested in another man. The musician did not wish to be monogamous and his love life was fluid and complex, but he enjoyed falling in love and allowed several relationships to last for months or years. After things had cooled with Tom Cothran, Bernstein fell for the journalist Robert Lee Kirkland III in the late 1970s, and a steady presence in his life throughout the 1980s was Aaron Stern, at the time dean of the American Conservatory of Music in Chicago, who had original ideas concerning education that Bernstein liked to discuss with him and also helped fund. Later, in 1988, Bernstein fell in love with Mark Stringer, a conducting student who went onto a major career, and his last paramour was Mark Adams Taylor, an aspiring novelist who described for Burton the fervency, romance, and 'Sheer poetry' that Bernstein brought to his pursuit of the young man.[29]

Bernstein was regularly feted during the 1980s with a bevy of major awards.[30] He received 22 honorary doctorates in his life, including seven during the 1980s: University of Warwick in England (1980), Johns Hopkins University (1980), Hebrew University in Israel (1981), Cleveland State University (1982), Boston University (1983), Pine Manor College (1987) and Fairfield University (1989). Major decorations from foreign governments started coming his way from the 1960s, and in the last decade of his life he added the rank of Commandeur in the French Legion of Honour in 1985 (having been named Chevalier in 1968 and Officier in 1978), the West German Commander's Cross of the Order of Merit in 1987, and Grand Order of Merit of the Italian Republic in 1988. In the United States he won a career achievement award from the Kennedy Center in 1980, was the initial fellow at the Indiana University Institute for Advanced Study in winter 1982 while working on *A Quiet Place*, won a special Grammy for lifetime achievement as a recording artist in 1985, and received the Gold Medal from the MacDowell Colony in 1987.

These are only a small sampling of the many honours that Bernstein received, but happiness or satisfaction for a rich and productive life seems to have largely eluded him in his last decade. Some of this resulted from a retreat from the progressivism seen in the United States and other countries. The election of Ronald Reagan as president in 1980 heralded a turn to the right and a hostile atmosphere for the arts that Bernstein found depressing; a pique with the American government finally led him to decline a National Medal for the Arts from President George H. W. Bush in response to the cancellation of arts grants that had supported controversial material. Bernstein also became alarmed by the rise of nationalism among conservative Jewish elements in Israel and what he saw as their persecution of the Palestinians, a remarkable turnaround for a man who had always been one of the nation's biggest supporters and who had a long record of cooperation with the Israel Philharmonic. After being raised in a progressive era and one who knew the repression of the left in the United States of the post-war era, Bernstein was dismayed to experience the politics of the 1980s.

But the personal malaise that Bernstein felt went well beyond political developments. Joan Peyser, a respected writer about music who had been editor of *Musical Quarterly*, met Bernstein while preparing an entry on him for *The New Grove Dictionary of American Music* (1985). She started to write a biography of the musician, and Bernstein cooperated with her along with his family, but when it became clear that Peyser was primarily interested in Bernstein's sexuality, they were far less sanguine about the project.[31] She spoke to a number of Bernstein's gay friends and some of his former lovers, however, and aspects of the book took an alarmingly homophobic turn, making it appear that Peyser believed that the most important purpose of her work was to ensure that Bernstein was outed in front of the whole world when she published her book in 1987. It is not a completely unbalanced account – she describes his musical genius and allows for his many successes – but the book includes errors and her portrayal of his personality is one-sided to the negative. In places Peyser seems to have believed that she was able to divine Bernstein's most intimate thoughts, and even admits that she used as a source a work of fiction that Bernstein allegedly in 1983 admitted had been based on his life.[32] Bernstein swore to his children that he would not read Peyser's book, but he certainly became aware that David Diamond was a major source for her, especially about Bernstein's sexuality. Two letters that ended their lifelong friendship make for painful reading.[33] Peyser is indeed correct that Bernstein's sexuality was a huge part of his personality and one of the major drives in his life, but the sensationalism and

Leonard Bernstein Place, adjacent to Lincoln Center in New York City, where Bernstein was music director of the New York Philharmonic from 1958–69.

The Watergate Hotel, adjacent to the Kennedy Center in Washington, DC, emblematic of the luxury hotels where Bernstein stayed when guest conducting and where the author of this book interviewed Bernstein on 15 March 1982.

homophobia that mark the book are unfortunate. Elsewhere in the media, Bernstein's portrayal in the 1980s ventured all over the map, from the relative encomium of an article by John Rockwell that appeared in the *New York Times Magazine* in August 1986 to conductor Leon Botstein's condemnation of what he considered the superficiality of Bernstein's conducting interpretations and compositions in *Harper's Magazine* from May 1983.[34] Rockwell's piece shows how many critics started to realize the importance of Bernstein's work late in his life while Botstein shows that there remained a part of musical intelligentsia that never accepted Bernstein and his popularizing of 'serious' music in both his conducting and composing.

Numerous interviews could be cited where Bernstein described his sadness as he aged, but perhaps more revealing is a poem that Burton cites that the musician wrote for his friend, poet and critic John Malcolm Brinnin (1916–1998), about a month after his seventieth birthday.[35] Entitled 'The Birthday Continues . . .', it is a rage against passing time and the process of being celebrated in one's old age. It is full of sexual imagery; Bernstein admits in the text that he physically enjoys the charms of young people, but in the end he is left alone, even while resisting becoming committed to yet another lover. It is a pitiable scream from a frustrated man who was aware of his own abilities but unfulfilled by his many successes and by his relentless pursuit of young male lovers.

   Serious health crises marked the last year of Bernstein's life, finally rendering him incapable of work for the last two months. As was his wont during the winter, he went to Key West in January 1990, where he loved to water ski and enjoy the weather with friends and family. The intention was to work on his opera with John Wells, but this proved difficult with many visitors, and to some Bernstein confessed that he did not feel his energy coming back in the way that he had become accustomed.[36] A return to New York from Europe in April 1990, where he had felt stabbing pain when breathing, preceded tests that found a malignant tumour in a membrane around the lung. Secret radiation treatment began, and then in June a reaction to tetracycline caused painful herpes outbreaks. He dealt with those and severe breathing difficulties while travelling to Japan for the Pacific Music Festival – a new event based around Bernstein – but ultimately he had to come home in July when he became too weak. He persevered through Tanglewood appearances, but when he returned to his Dakota apartment in New York he found that doctors had taken over. He spent his birthday later that month in the hospital being dried out from alcohol and the many drugs he had been self-administering – including dangerous painkillers – but later for a time he could retreat to his home in Fairfield, where he could be free of medical domination. When fibrosis developed in his lungs he had to return to New York, and soon he was getting around in a wheelchair. His friend

Dr Kevin Cahill, who had treated Bernstein when he contracted amoebic dysentery in Mexico in 1979, was as close as the musician had to a personal physician, but he had always been reluctant to place himself under the care of a single doctor. Friends and family came and went but Bernstein, having great trouble breathing and in constant pain, seemed obsessed with impending death. It came on 14 October while Cahill was giving him an injection, caused by a heart attack that the physician said was brought on by emphysema, a pleural tumour and pulmonary infections. Not long before Bernstein had announced his retirement from conducting, alerting many to his serious condition. After his death the musical world went into overdrive in eulogies and tributes. Bernstein was buried in Green-Wood Cemetery in Brooklyn next to his wife, Felicia, the woman that he loved and the person who seems to have most successfully helped him cope with his demons.

8

A Final Evaluation

Leonard Bernstein was a complicated man. When he found a friend he would form a close bond and often would keep in touch with the person for years, but he could also be tactless and overbearing in public and private situations. He was a homosexual with a powerful libido who had many male lovers, including several with whom he formed lasting relationships, but he forged his closest bond with his wife of many years, actress Felicia Montealegre Bernstein. The union produced three children who were very important to him and with whom he was close until his death. His marriage might have been partly motivated by appearances, making possible professional opportunities that would have been harder to attain for an obviously gay man, but his love and passion for Felicia were real. His decision to marry was also an expression of his Jewish upbringing, where family life and children are very important. His religious background was significant to him, but his actual practice as a Jew extended mostly to the high holy days, and his dedication to psychoanalysis perhaps informed him more than religion about his inner life. He spoke often about a modern 'crisis of faith', but seldom defined what he meant by that. Judaism made him a strong supporter of Israel. An area where Bernstein showed fewer contradictions was in politics, where he remained progressive through several contrasting eras, and his concern for human rights led him to doubt the conservative direction that Israeli politics moved in the 1980s, when the rights of Palestinians seemed more threatened. He had an outsized ego and craved adoration and attention, but he was a generous teacher and mentor to young musicians. In addition to his musical gifts, Bernstein was a polymath who spoke several languages, a brilliant pedagogue, memorable writer and convincing speaker. There would seem to have been many fields where he might have excelled, but his discovery of music in his youth guided all of his professional ambitions, and he steadfastly refused to choose one area in the field in which to work.

Few musicians could match the range of Bernstein's musical gifts. He had the ear and innate musicality to understand very complicated scores, and he was a fine pianist. His rhythmic sense was superb and he had extensive knowledge of music history from at least the late Baroque to the present. He was an excellent analyst who easily made associations between music and other fields. His ability to explain musical concepts at multiple levels was extraordinary. As a conductor, along with the New York Philharmonic, he formed one of the most productive associations with an orchestra in the history of the art, but he was only the group's music director for eleven years. The remainder of his conducting career was almost entirely as a guest, including fruitful relationships with the Vienna Philharmonic, Israel Philharmonic and Boston Symphony Orchestra, among other ensembles. His great popularity in Vienna, as an American conductor often leading Austrian and German compositions, was remarkable. His range as a conductor grew until he had embraced a large part of the Western classical canon. Like most conductors, his interpretations were subjective, but he developed wide-ranging specialities and interests: Haydn, Beethoven, Schumann, Berlioz, Wagner, Mahler, Ives, Stravinsky, Copland, Gershwin and a number of other composers with whom he became associated in compelling performances. He had a special gift for bringing to life American music and twentieth-century works, but he tended to avoid the avant-garde.

A Bernstein concert was an event, perhaps variably described by the critics, but audiences loved his charisma and commitment to music. His conducting motions were large and demonstrative and often criticized, but they were part of his personality and a sincere expression of his reaction to the music. The hundreds of audio and video recordings that Bernstein made, many of which remain commercially viable, constitute one of the largest such legacies of the twentieth century. His energetic work as a musical educator on television is unique in the mass-media era. The number of people, old and young, that Bernstein turned on to classical music can hardly be calculated, but it is safe to say that his importance to the classical musical world in the twentieth century was foundational.

Bernstein's legacy as a composer rests most securely on the place of *West Side Story* as one of the icons of American culture in the middle of the twentieth century – a status that disappointed a man obsessed with writing serious, concert works that would be perceived as important – but his output is one of the more varied

Bernstein's grave in Green-Wood Cemetery, Brooklyn, NY, where admirers apparently come to bring decorations, pencils for the composer and the odd guitar pick.

of the twentieth century. *West Side Story* is a score of unusual beauty and profundity for the popular theatre, but Bernstein's other Broadway musicals show his gifts as a composer of musical comedy songs in *On the Town* and *Wonderful Town*, and *Candide* is a brilliant expression of his natural eclecticism and talent as a parodist. For a composer who completed only five Broadway scores, his importance in the genre is most unusual. In other types of dramatic compositions he made a distinctive contribution in his single film score, *On the Waterfront*, and among his three ballets with Jerome Robbins, *Fancy Free* is one of the best ballet scores by an American composer. The opera *Trouble in Tahiti* offers fascinating commentary on the American consumerist culture and growth of suburbs around 1950. *Mass* is a work that could define 'unique', and it is also one of the most revealing documents that the man left concerning himself and his feelings about the world around him. Despite its size and controversial aspects, and the expense of mounting it, *Mass* remains a possible work of choice for performing institutions trying to make a statement. While many critics could not accept Bernstein's wide-ranging eclecticism in his concert music, the way that he mixed classical idioms with jazz, blues and other popular idioms that he also loved is quintessentially American and resulted in several works that have remained in the repertory. *Chichester Psalms* and the *Serenade after Plato's 'Symposium'*, his violin concerto, might be his most important contributions to classical music, but his three symphonies, especially the 'Jeremiah' and 'The Age of Anxiety', are thoroughly professional contributions to the genre. His Symphony no. 3, 'Kaddish', is more personal and difficult, but a valuable window into what made the man tick. When one considers his first and third symphonies along with a few other pieces, Bernstein emerges as one of the most significant composers of Jewish works in the history of Western music. In terms of his style, he wrote memorable melodies, rhythms that make one's body want to move, and orchestrated with the best of them.

I had the good fortune of seeing Bernstein in person two times. In spring 1976 I saw him inaugurate his Bicentennial tour with the New York Philharmonic in Carnegie Hall, a striking programme where, among other works, he led Gershwin's *Rhapsody in Blue* from the piano. This young musician was enthralled by that performance, which encapsulated almost everything that I thought at the time was great about American music. Then in 1981, while working on my master's thesis on the influence of Copland on Bernstein, I wrote Bernstein a letter requesting an interview. Months passed, but in winter 1982 I heard from Helen Coates, his long-time secretary, with an invitation to watch Bernstein lead a rehearsal with the National Symphony in Washington, DC, and then speak with him afterwards. On 15 March, I watched him rehearse the ensemble in Elgar's *Enigma Variations*, Walton's Viola Concerto with New York Philharmonic violist Sol Greitzer, and his own *Halil* with Philharmonic flautist Julius Baker. Bernstein rehearsed, cajoled, taught, demanded, entreated and danced that afternoon, a master musician at the top of his game. His embrace and understanding of the music was total – whatever else could have been said about Bernstein, there was no doubting his commitment to the music that he performed. After the rehearsal, while still at the Kennedy Center, Bernstein asked if I had heard any Copland influence in *Halil*, a new piece that I did not know well. I replied with terrible naivety: 'Yes, in the jazz-like section.' He snapped back, 'That's not jazz-like!', my first lesson about taking great care when talking with composers about their music. I also found out that I had a great deal to learn about what Bernstein considered to be jazz.

I rode with Bernstein in his limousine around the corner to the Watergate Hotel, where he had a large suite. It was there that I experienced the man's laser-like concentration, described by a number of commentators. He made you feel as if you were the most important person in the world while in his presence, an intoxicating feeling. Despite our rough start, we talked for more than an hour, with him asking me perhaps half as many questions as I asked him. He gave me a few interesting quotations about what he perceived to be Copland's influence on him and made some fascinating remarks about eclecticism, the most revealing part of the interview in terms of his own music, which many critics pejoratively described as eclectic. Bernstein stated that he thought 'every composer is eclectic to some extent', because, in the case of a famous German composer, there was 'This combination of Haydn, Mozart, and Bach, and everything else that goes into making up Beethoven, plus the magic factor which is the individuated thing we call Beethoven.'[1] Bernstein placed himself in a long line of what he considered to be eclectic composers, also naming Bach and Stravinsky, whom he called 'the most eclectic composer that ever lived'.[2] Some might dismiss such a statement as the delusions of a defensive composer, but I have come to see it as a glimpse behind Bernstein's compositional curtain. He was a very thoughtful musician who knew huge swaths of repertory and who had influenced whom, even if he sometimes overstated that influence. Bernstein was able to write music in any style that might be necessary. This did not stop him from developing his own style, but all of the conducting and his remarkable musical memory came with a price, complicating the act of composition for him as he searched for ideas that he could identify as his own. He perhaps assumed that other composers had similar struggles, but Bernstein talked about it a lot. His struggle between conducting and composing, which he often spoke about, demonstrated his open, confessional nature, something I also experienced during the interview. He talked a bit that day about homosexuality and marriage, reflecting on those possibilities in my life, but clearly it was something that he had thought about a great deal.

As I left that suite at the Watergate Hotel, my head was swimming. I had had a remarkably personal conversation with one of the most famous men in the field in which I hoped to work, and I was a mere babe in arms by comparison. For whatever reason, this man granted me what felt like an audience, and at times spoke to me like someone he had known for years. It might have been an attempted seduction – many of his lovers were young – but even if it was, it was a generous expenditure of his time and that discussion is part of what has made me remain interested in the man for more than three decades. I learned at first hand that Leonard Bernstein was many things, including an exceptionally memorable man.

References

1 'Safe at the Piano': Bernstein's Youth, 1918–39

1 The quotation in the chapter title is from Allen Shawn, *Leonard Bernstein: An American Musician* (New Haven, CT, 2014), p. 22.
2 The most complete account of Leonard Bernstein's family background and childhood appears in Humphrey Burton, *Leonard Bernstein* (New York, 1994), pp. 3–18.
3 Ibid., p. 9, and Jonathan D. Sarna, 'Leonard Bernstein and the Boston Jewish Community of His Youth', *Journal of the Society for American Music*, III/1 (2009), pp. 35–9.
4 Burton, *Leonard Bernstein*, p. 17.
5 Shawn, *Leonard Bernstein*, p. 22.
6 Burton, *Leonard Bernstein*, p. 26.
7 Shawn, *Leonard Bernstein*, p. 29.
8 For biographical material on Ramin, see Steven Suskin, *The Sound of Broadway Music: A Book of Orchestrators and Orchestrations* (Oxford and New York, 2009), pp. 72–8.
9 Shawn, *Leonard Bernstein*, p. 37.
10 To consult Bernstein's thesis, see Leonard Bernstein, *Findings* (New York, 1982), pp. 36–99.
11 For consideration of Bernstein's thesis in the context of his career, see Geoffrey Block, 'Bernstein's Senior Thesis at Harvard: The Roots of a Lifelong Search to Discover an American Identity', *College Music Symposium*, XLVIII (2008), pp. 52–68.
12 See Copland's letter from 7 December 1938 in Nigel Simeone, *The Leonard Bernstein Letters* (New Haven, CT, 2013), pp. 25–6.
13 Shawn, *Leonard Bernstein*, p. 36.

14 For a list of Bernstein's compositions by genre, see Paul R. Laird and Hsun Lin, *Leonard Bernstein: A Research and Information Guide*, 2nd edn, Routledge Music Bibliographies (New York, 2015), pp. 49–75.

15 Bernstein's three articles for *Modern Music* were 'Forecast and Review: Boston Carries On', XV/4 (1938), pp. 239–41; 'Forecast and Review: Season of Premieres in Boston', XVI/2 (1939), pp. 103–6; and 'Forecast and Review: The Latest from Boston', XVI/3 (1939), pp. 182–4.

16 It is striking to see with what ease and intimacy Mitropoulos wrote to the young Bernstein. See Simeone, *The Leonard Bernstein Letters*, pp. 21–2, 28.

17 Personal interview with Leonard Bernstein by the author, Washington, DC, 15 March 1982.

18 Burton, *Leonard Bernstein*, p. 53.

19 Howard Pollack, *Marc Blitzstein: His Life, His Work, His World* (New York, 2012), p. 184.

20 Shawn, *Leonard Bernstein*, p. 44.

21 Barry Seldes, *Leonard Bernstein: The Political Life of an American Musician* (Berkeley, CA, 2009), p. 24.

22 Burton, *Leonard Bernstein*, pp. 28–30.

23 Joan Peyser, 'The Bernstein Legacy', *Opera News*, LXV/1 (2000), p. 23. Peyser also makes Bernstein's potent libido a major part of her biography, *Bernstein: A Biography* (New York, 1987).

2 'The Spirit of Koussevitzky':
Bernstein Discovers Conducting, 1939–43

1 The quotation in this chapter title appears in Humphrey Burton, *Leonard Bernstein* (New York, 1994), p. 78.

2 Bernstein reported this to Copland in a letter from 9 August 1939. See Nigel Simeone, *The Leonard Bernstein Letters* (New Haven, CT, 2013), pp. 34–5.

3 Meryle Secrest, *Leonard Bernstein: A Life* (New York, 1994), p. 60.

4 Ibid., p. 66.

5 Ibid., p. 67.

6 Burton, *Leonard Bernstein*, p. 67.

7   Ibid., p. 65. Also, Helen Coates wrote Bernstein a letter on 14 October
    1939 in which she asked Bernstein if he had decided to accept 'D. M.'s
    . . . offer to finance you this year?' See Simeone, *The Leonard Bernstein
    Letters*, p. 37.

8   Burton, *Leonard Bernstein*, p. 67.

9   Ibid., pp. 69–70.

10 Simeone, *The Leonard Bernstein Letters*, p. 45.

11 Ibid., p. 582.

12 Joseph Horowitz, 'Koussevitzky, Serge (Alexandrovich)', in *The Grove
    Dictionary of American Music*, ed. Charles Hiroshi Garrett (New York,
    2013), vol. IV, p. 661.

13 Secrest, *Leonard Bernstein*, p. 37.

14 Burton, *Leonard Bernstein*, p. 76.

15 Ibid., p. 78.

16 Ibid. Bernstein published his opening remarks for Tanglewood from
    8 July 1970, including this remark, in Leonard Bernstein, *Findings*
    (New York, 1982), pp. 273–84.

17 Burton, *Leonard Bernstein*, p. 81.

18 Simeone, *The Leonard Bernstein Letters*, p. 65.

19 Burton, *Leonard Bernstein*, p. 88.

20 Simeone, *The Leonard Bernstein Letters*, p. 69.

21 Burton, *Leonard Bernstein*, pp. 93–4.

22 Ibid., p. 94.

23 Simeone, *The Leonard Bernstein Letters*, p. 81.

24 Ibid., p. 84.

25 Burton, *Leonard Bernstein*, p. 96.

26 Simeone, *The Leonard Bernstein Letters*, p. 86.

27 Secrest, *Leonard Bernstein*, pp. 85–90, 94–6.

28 Simeone, *The Leonard Bernstein Letters*, p. 137.

29 See Lars Helgert, 'The Songs of Leonard Bernstein and Charles Stern
    in 1942: Toward the Origins of Bernstein as a Dramatic Composer',
    American Music Research Center Journal, XXI (2012), pp. 41–66.

30 'Frau' appears often in references in correspondence with both
    Oppenheim and Copland. A telling reference concerning Bernstein
    and his progress with the doctor appears in Bernstein's letter to
    Oppenheim on 12 July 1943. See Simeone, *The Leonard Bernstein Letters*,
    p. 133.

31 Burton, *Leonard Bernstein*, p. 109. Letters from Bernstein to Copland that Burton quotes before this delightful response from Copland are extraordinarily revealing of the chaotic personal life Bernstein led at this time.

32 Allen Shawn, *Leonard Bernstein: An American Musician* (New Haven, CT, 2014), pp. 52–3.

33 Simeone, *The Leonard Bernstein Letters*, p. 116.

34 Ibid., p. 128.

35 Jack Gottlieb, 'Symbols of Faith in the Music of Leonard Bernstein', *Musical Quarterly*, LXVI/2 (April 1980), pp. 292–3.

36 Simeone, *The Leonard Bernstein Letters*, p. 111.

3 'I have a fine large apartment in Carnegie Hall':
A Time of Searching, 1943–51

1 The quotation in the chapter title is from Nigel Simeone, *The Leonard Bernstein Letters* (New Haven, CT, 2013), p. 145.

2 Olin Downes, 'Bernstein Shows Mastery of Score', *New York Times*, 15 November 1943, p. 40.

3 Humphrey Burton, *Leonard Bernstein* (New York, 1994), p. 117.

4 Ibid., p. 122.

5 Allen Shawn, *Leonard Bernstein: An American Musician* (New Haven, CT, 2014), p. 60.

6 Burton, *Leonard Bernstein*, p. 124.

7 Ibid., p. 127.

8 Simeone, *The Leonard Bernstein Letters*, p. 150.

9 Ibid., p. 151.

10 Ibid., p. 156.

11 Ibid., p. 154.

12 Ibid., p. 155.

13 Ibid., p. 157.

14 For the definitive study of *On the Town*, see Carol J. Oja, *Bernstein Meets Broadway: Collaborative Art in a Time of War* (New York, 2014).

15 For more on George Abbott, see Paul R. Laird, 'More Than a Producer: "George Abbott Presents"', in Laura MacDonald and William A.

Everett, *The Palgrave Handbook of Musical Theatre Producers* (New York, 2017), pp. 163–72.

16 For the director's take on the creation of *On the Town*, see George Abbott, *Mister Abbott* (New York, 1963), pp. 199–200.

17 For the remarkable story of a Japanese American dancer starring on Broadway during the Second World War, see Sono Osato, *Distant Dances* (New York, 1980), pp. 229–47.

18 Lewis Nichols, 'The Play: "On the Town"', *New York Times*, 29 December 1944, p. 11.

19 See www.ibdb.com, accessed 9 August 2016.

20 See Barry Seldes, *Leonard Bernstein: The Political Life of an American Musician* (Berkeley, CA, 2009), pp. 25–32, for coverage of this portion of Bernstein's career.

21 Burton, *Leonard Bernstein*, p. 138.

22 'Bernstein to Lead the City Symphony', *New York Times*, 29 August 1945, p. 25.

23 Ruth Orkin, 'In the World of Music: The New York City Symphony to Inaugurate Its Season', *New York Times*, 7 October 1945, p. X4.

24 Olin Downes, 'Bernstein Opens at the City Center: Conducts in Brilliant Manner Shostakovich First Symphony – Finds Improved Orchestra', *New York Times*, 9 October 1945, p. 25.

25 Burton, *Leonard Bernstein*, p. 144.

26 H[oward] T[aubman], 'Bernstein Leads Three Premieres: Goodman Brilliant as Soloist in North's Revue at City Center Program of Contrasts', *New York Times*, 19 November 1946, p. 48.

27 Olin Downes, 'Audience Cheers Blitzstein Work: Throng at City Center Strong in Approval of "Airborne" at Its World Premiere', *New York Times*, 2 April 1946, p. 23.

28 Quoted in Burton, *Leonard Bernstein*, p. 169.

29 'Bernstein Resigns as Symphony Head: Conductor Leaves City Group Because of Expected Cut in Budget for the Fall', *New York Times*, 8 March 1948, p. 17.

30 Quoted in Erica K. Argyropoulos, 'Conducting Culture: Leonard Bernstein, the Israel Philharmonic Orchestra, and the Negotiation of Jewish American Identity, 1947–1967', PhD dissertation, University of Kansas (2015), p. 77.

31 Ibid., pp. 85–6.

32 Simeone, *The Leonard Bernstein Letters*, pp. 224–5.

33 Burton, *Leonard Bernstein*, p. 162.

34 Argyropoulos, 'Conducting Culture', pp. 91–2.

35 Peter Gradenwitz, 'Palestine Visitor: Bernstein Helps Celebrate Orchestra's Anniversary', *New York Times*, 18 May 1947, p. 87.

36 Simeone, *The Leonard Bernstein Letters*, pp. 225–6.

37 For example, see ibid., p. 228, where a letter from 23 July 1947 by Bernstein's analyst, Marketa Morris, describes how the musician apparently needs male companionship the same day that he saw Felicia.

38 Simeone, *The Leonard Bernstein Letters*, p. 214.

39 Burton, *Leonard Bernstein*, pp. 167, 171.

40 John Martin, '"Facsimile" Ballet Has Premiere Here: Robbins' New Work, Given by Theatre Group, Sees Creator Turning to Serious Ends', *New York Times*, 25 October 1946, p. 36.

41 Simeone, *The Leonard Bernstein Letters*, p. 215.

42 Burton, *Leonard Bernstein*, p. 167.

43 Simeone, *The Leonard Bernstein Letters*, p. 231.

44 Ibid., p. 232.

45 Burton, *Leonard Bernstein*, pp. 190–91.

46 Shawn, *Leonard Bernstein*, pp. 95–9.

47 Ibid., p. 96.

48 Quoted ibid., p. 93.

49 Jack Gottlieb, 'Symbols of Faith in the Music of Leonard Bernstein', *Musical Quarterly*, LXVI/2 (1980), pp. 287–92.

50 Burton, *Leonard Bernstein*, p. 195.

51 Ibid.

52 Simeone, *The Leonard Bernstein Letters*, pp. 268–70.

53 Leonard Bernstein, *'Peter Pan' from the Play by J. M. Barrie*, Linda Eder/ Daniel Narducci/Amber Chamber Orchestra conducted by Alexander Frey (Koch International Classics 7596, 2005), CD. Songs from the score that have become known include 'Build My House', 'Neverland' and 'Dream with Me'.

54 Burton, *Leonard Bernstein*, p. 172.

55 Argyropoulos, 'Conducting Culture', pp. 111–12.

56 Ibid., p. 122.

57 Ibid., p. 139.

58 Ibid., pp. 123, 126–7.

59 Ibid., pp. 133–5.
60 Ibid., p. 136.
61 Ibid., pp. 140–41.
62 Ibid., pp. 141–6.
63 Burton, *Leonard Bernstein*, p. 193.
64 Olin Downes, 'Bernstein Leads Messiaen's Work', *New York Times*,
    11 December 1949, p. 87.
65 Simeone, *The Leonard Bernstein Letters*, p. 271.
66 Argyropoulos, 'Conducting Culture', p. 153.
67 Simeone, *The Leonard Bernstein Letters*, p. 283.
68 Burton, *Leonard Bernstein*, p. 206.
69 Simeone, *The Leonard Bernstein Letters*, pp. 271–2.
70 Burton, *Leonard Bernstein*, pp. 208–10.
71 Simeone, *The Leonard Bernstein Letters*, p. 266.
72 Ibid., p. 290.
73 Ibid., p. 291.
74 Burton, *Leonard Bernstein*, p. 214.
75 Simeone, *The Leonard Bernstein Letters*, pp. 293–4.

4 'I simply must decide what I'm going to be when I grow up':
   Leaning Towards Composition, 1952–7

1 The quotation in this chapter title is from Nigel Simeone, *The Leonard
   Bernstein Letters* (New Haven, CT, 2013), p. 337.
2 Allen Shawn, *Leonard Bernstein: An American Musician* (New Haven, CT,
   2014), p. 137.
3 See Humphrey Burton, *Leonard Bernstein* (New York, 1994), pp. 220–21,
   for a detailed description of the festival.
4 Ibid., p. 229.
5 See Jack Gottlieb, '*Candide* Goes to College', in *Working with Bernstein:
   A Memoir* (New York, 2010), pp. 167–71.
6 Simeone, *The Leonard Bernstein Letters*, p. 295.
7 Burton, *Leonard Bernstein*, p. 221.
8 Olin Downes, 'TANGLEWOOD IDEALS: Principles of Berkshire Music
   Center Adhere to Koussevitzky's Standards', *New York Times*, 17 August
   1952, p. X7.

9 See, for example, Burton, *Leonard Bernstein*, p. 232.

10 Leonard Bernstein, Betty Comden and Adolph Green, *Wonderful Town* (New York, 2004), p. 10.

11 George Abbott, *Mister Abbott* (New York, 1963), p. 233.

12 Brooks Atkinson, 'At the Theatre', *New York Times*, 26 February 1953, p. 22.

13 Bernstein, Comden and Green, *Wonderful Town*, p. 172.

14 Howard Pollack, *Aaron Copland: The Life and Work of an Uncommon Man* (Urbana and Chicago, IL, 1999), pp. 454–7.

15 See Barry Seldes, *Leonard Bernstein: The Political Life of an American Musician* (Berkeley, CA, 2009), pp. 69–72, and Simeone, *The Leonard Bernstein Letters*, pp. 298–309, quotation on p. 306.

16 Simeone, *The Leonard Bernstein Letters*, p. 310.

17 Greg Lawrence, *Dance with Demons: The Life of Jerome Robbins* (New York, 2001), pp. 199–211.

18 For a description of this visit to Israel, see Erica K. Argyropoulos, 'Conducting Culture: Leonard Bernstein, the Israel Philharmonic Orchestra, and the Negotiation of Jewish American Identity, 1947–1967', PhD dissertation, University of Kansas (2015), pp. 172–4.

19 Stephen Lias, 'A Comparison of Leonard Bernstein's Incidental Music for the Film *On the Waterfront* and Subsequent *Symphonic Suite* from the Film, and an Original Composition: Symphony no. 1 – "Music for the Theater"', DMA document, Louisiana State University (1997), p. 7.

20 Anthony Bushard, *Leonard Bernstein's 'On the Waterfront': A Film Score Guide* (Lanham, MD, 2013), pp. 51ff.

21 Anthony Bushard, 'From *On the Waterfront* to *West Side Story*, or There's Nowhere Like Somewhere', *Studies in Musical Theatre*, III/1 (2009), pp. 61–75.

22 Leonard Bernstein, 'Interlude: Upper Dubbing, Calif.', in *The Joy of Music* (New York, 1959), pp. 65–9.

23 Lias, 'A Comparison', p. 85.

24 Burton, *Leonard Bernstein*, pp. 238, 386. Bernstein left the project long before the completion of *Brother Sun, Sister Moon*.

25 Ibid., p. 239.

26 Shawn, *Leonard Bernstein*, pp. 123–7.

27 Leonard Bernstein, 'Program Notes', in *Serenade after Plato's 'Symposium' for Solo Violin, Strings, Harp and Percussion* (New York, 1988), p. [iii].

28 Howard Taubman, 'TOUCH OF CLASS ON TV: Music Rarely Fares Well, But It Did with Bernstein, Reiner and Mozart', *New York Times*, 21 November 1954, p. X7.

29 Burton, *Leonard Bernstein*, p. 252.

30 Leonard Bernstein, 'American Musical Comedy', in *The Joy of Music* (New York, 1959), pp. 164–91, quotation on p. 191.

31 Shawn, *Leonard Bernstein*, p. 134.

32 Simeone, *The Leonard Bernstein Letters*, p. 311.

33 Ibid., p. 316.

34 Burton, *Leonard Bernstein*, p. 257.

35 Simeone, *The Leonard Bernstein Letters*, p. 352.

36 Ibid.

37 Ibid., p. 319.

38 Tyrone Guthrie, *A Life in the Theatre* (New York, 1959), pp. 240–41.

39 Brooks Atkinson, 'Musical "Candide": Lillian Hellman and Leonard Bernstein Turn Voltaire Satire into Fine Play', *New York Times*, 9 December 1956, p. 149.

40 See Helen Smith, *There's a Place For Us: The Musical Theatre Works of Leonard Bernstein* (Farnham, 2011), pp. 99–138.

41 William A. Everett, '*Candide* and the Tradition of American Operetta', *Studies in Musical Theatre*, III/1 (2009), pp. 53–9, and Shawn, *Leonard Bernstein*, p. 137.

42 Andrew Porter, '*Candide*: An Introduction', pp. 8–14 of programme booklet from Leonard Bernstein, *Candide*, London Symphony Orchestra and Chorus/Bernstein (Deutsche Grammophon 429 734–2, 1991), CD.

43 Among many sources on the show, two excellent studies that look at different aspects are Nigel Simeone, *Leonard Bernstein: 'West Side Story'*, Landmarks in Music since 1950 (London, 2009); and Elizabeth A. Wells, *'West Side Story': Cultural Perspectives on an American Musical* (Lanham, MD, 2011).

44 Burton, *Leonard Bernstein*, p. 248.

45 Simeone, *'West Side Story'*, pp. 21–6.

46 Ibid., p. 31, and Burton, *Leonard Bernstein*, pp. 256–7.

47 Library of Congress, Leonard Bernstein Collection, Box 75/5. Simeone, *'West Side Story'*, deals with this source on p. 45. Carol Lawrence describes her audition process and her joint audition with Kert in her interview in William Westbrook Burton, *Conversations About Bernstein* (New York, 1995), pp. 174–7.

48 For example, see ibid., pp. 172, 177–8.

49 See Simeone, *'West Side Story'*, pp. 85–92, for consideration of the orchestration.

50 Ibid., p. 63.

51 Burton, *Leonard Bernstein*, pp. 274–5.

52 Seldes, *Leonard Bernstein*, pp. 72–86.

53 Burton, *Leonard Bernstein*, p. 254.

54 'BERNSTEIN NAMED BY PHILHARMONIC: Will Share Responsibility of Orchestra With Mitropoulos in the 1957–58 Season', *New York Times*, 16 October 1956, p. 36.

55 Shawn, *Leonard Bernstein*, p. 141.

56 'Wunderkind', *Time*, LXIX/5 (4 February 1957), p. 72.

57 Simeone, *The Leonard Bernstein Letters*, pp. 364–5.

58 Ross Parmenter, 'Leonard Bernstein Heads Philharmonic', *New York Times*, 20 November 1957, p. 1.

59 See William R. Trotter, *Priest of Music: The Life of Dimitri Mitropoulos* (Portland, OR, 1995), p. 241, 396. Trotter notes that Bernstein contributed to Mitropoulos's failure to succeed Koussevitzky in Boston by offering testimony of the Greek conductor's homosexuality, and that he contributed to Mitropoulos's losing the New York Philharmonic with a similar role.

5 'I'm going to be a conductor, after all!':
Philharmonic Maestro, 1957–69

1 The quotation in the chapter title is from Nigel Simeone, *The Leonard Bernstein Letters* (New Haven, CT, 2013), p. 363.

2 Humphrey Burton, *Leonard Bernstein* (New York, 1994), p. 291.

3 Harold C. Schonberg, 'New Job for the Protean Mr. Bernstein: The Philharmonic Poses a Challenge for Music's Jack-of-all-trades', *New York Times*, 22 December 1957, p. 120.

4   Burton, *Leonard Bernstein*, p. 294.

5   Schonberg, 'New Job for the Protean Mr. Bernstein', p. 120.

6   Burton, *Leonard Bernstein*, p. 350.

7   Allen Shawn, *Leonard Bernstein: An American Musician* (New Haven, CT, 2014), pp. 190–95.

8   Carlos Moseley, 'THE PHILHARMONIC HATH CHARMS: It Has Proved Itself a Cultural Emissary In Latin America', *New York Times*, 25 May 1958, p. X9.

9   Ibid.

10 Burton, *Leonard Bernstein*, p. 288.

11 Michael James, 'Philharmonic Flies on Long Foreign Tour: Group Will Perform in the Soviet Union on 10-week Trip', *New York Times*, 4 August 1959, p. 3.

12 Burton, *Leonard Bernstein*, p. 305.

13 Ibid., p. 308.

14 Osgood Caruthers, 'Moscow Cheers Bernstein at Philharmonic Triumph: RUSSIANS STIRRED BY PHILHARMONIC', *New York Times*, 23 August 1959, p. 1.

15 Osgood Caruthers, 'Bernstein, on Birthday, Leads Orchestra in 2 Stravinsky Works: "The Sacre" Cheered Wildly in Moscow – Composer Feted With Parties and Gifts', *New York Times*, 26 August 1959, p. 25.

16 Max Frankel, 'RUSSIANS STIRRED BY PHILHARMONIC: Warmest Reception Given at 3d Concert – Bernstein to Talk on Podium Today', *New York Times*, 25 August 1959, p. 36.

17 Caruthers, 'Bernstein, on Birthday'.

18 Burton, *Leonard Bernstein*, p. 311.

19 Ibid., p. 307.

20 Ibid., p. 308.

21 Harold C. Schonberg, 'Philharmonic Back at Carnegie Hall', *New York Times*, 21 May 1976, p. 69; Flora Lewis, 'An American in Paris, Leonard Bernstein Enchants the City With a Gershwin Melody', *New York Times*, 19 June 1976, p. 50; John Rockwell, 'Music: Philharmonic Plays to 50,000: Ends 32-concert Tour in Sheep Meadow Bernstein in 3 Roles on All-American Bill', *New York Times*, 5 July 1976, p. 5.

22 See, for example, Alicia Kopfstein-Penk, *Leonard Bernstein and His Young People's Concerts* (Lanham, MD, 2015).

23 Jack Gottlieb, compiler, *Leonard Bernstein: A Complete Catalogue of His Works, Celebrating His 60th Birthday, August 25, 1978* (New York, 1978), p. 54.

24 Burton, *Leonard Bernstein*, p. 329.

25 Leonard Bernstein, *The Joy of Music* (New York, 1959).

26 Leonard Bernstein, *The Infinite Variety of Music* (New York, 1966); Leonard Bernstein, *Leonard Bernstein's Young People's Concerts* (New York, 1961, revd and expanded edn, 1970).

27 James H. North, *New York Philharmonic, The Authorized Recordings, 1917–2005: A Discography* (Lanham, MD, 2006), pp. 122–3.

28 Ibid., pp. 268–9.

29 Ibid., pp. 344–56.

30 Burton, *Leonard Bernstein*, p. 303.

31 Howard Taubman, 'The Philharmonic – What's Wrong With It And Why', *New York Times*, 29 April 1956, p. 139.

32 Burton, *Leonard Bernstein*, p. 293.

33 Ibid.

34 Harold C. Schonberg, 'SPREADING THIN: Bernstein's Many Activities Leave Minimum Time for Regular Season', *New York Times*, 16 April 1961, p. X9.

35 Ibid.

36 Harold C. Schonberg, 'Music: Inner Voices of Glenn Gould, Pianist Plays Them in Addition to Brahms, Bernstein Speech Hints at the Interpretation', *New York Times*, 7 April 1962, p. 17.

37 Shawn, *Leonard Bernstein*, pp. 202–3.

38 Harold C. Schonberg, 'Bernstein Given A Hero's Farewell – End of His Formal Duties May Bring Busier Life', *New York Times*, 19 May 1969, p. 2/54.

39 Papers of John F. Kennedy. Presidential Papers. White House Staff Files of Sanford L. Fox. Social Events, 1961–1964. Events: 11 May 1962, Dinner, André Malraux of France. Seating plan, detail.

40 Burton, *Leonard Bernstein*, p. 320.

41 Ibid., p. 341.

42 Harold C. Schonberg, 'Opera: "Falstaff" Staged by Zeffirelli', *New York Times*, 7 March 1964, p. 12.

43 Paul R. Laird, *The Chichester Psalms of Leonard Bernstein*, CMS Sourcebooks in American Music (Hillsdale, NY, 2010), pp. 9–12.

44 Simeone, *The Leonard Bernstein Letters*, pp. 464–5.

45 Leonard Bernstein, 'What I Thought . . . What I Did', *New York Times*, 24 October 1965, p. 2/17.

46 Burton, *Leonard Bernstein*, p. 353.

47 Shawn, *Leonard Bernstein*, p. 206.

48 John Gruen, *The Private World of Leonard Bernstein* (New York, 1968).

49 Burton, *Leonard Bernstein*, p. 378.

50 Ibid., pp. 373–4.

51 Shawn, *Leonard Bernstein*, p. 186.

52 Both quotations appear in 'ISRAEL APPLAUDS BERNSTEIN WORK: He Conducts at Premiere of Symphony in Tel Aviv', *New York Times*, 11 December 1962, p. 55.

53 Simeone, *The Leonard Bernstein Letters*, p. 460.

54 Ross Parmenter, 'Music: Bernstein's Symphony no. 3: Premiere of "Kaddish" Given in Boston', *New York Times*, 1 February 1964, p. 12.

55 Burton, *Leonard Bernstein*, p. 336.

56 Shawn, *Leonard Bernstein*, p. 188.

57 See Laird, *The Chichester Psalms of Leonard Bernstein*.

58 Burton, *Leonard Bernstein*, p. 349.

59 Hussey wrote this in a letter to Bernstein dated 14 August 1964. See Laird, *The Chichester Psalms of Leonard Bernstein*, pp. 22–3.

6 'I do know that the answer is *Yes*': Living with Fame, 1969–78

1 The quotation in the chapter title is from Leonard Bernstein, *The Unanswered Question: Six Talks at Harvard* (Cambridge, MA, 1976), p. 425.

2 Humphrey Burton, *Leonard Bernstein* (New York, 1994), p. 358.

3 Ibid., pp. 386–7.

4 Ibid., p. 388. The author refers to statements that Bernstein made in a *Young People's Concert* at about this time.

5 Harold C. Schonberg, 'Music: Concert "Fidelio": Bernstein Conducts the Philharmonic', *New York Times*, 16 January 1970, p. 32.

6 Burton, *Leonard Bernstein*, p. 390.

7 Charlotte Curtis, 'Black Panther Philosophy Is Debated at the Bernsteins'', *New York Times*, 15 January 1970, p. 48.

8 'False Note on Black Panthers', *New York Times*, 16 January 1970, p. 38.

9 Tom Wolfe's essay first appeared in *New York* magazine (June 1970) and he reprinted it in his *Radical Chic and Mau-Mauing the Flak Catchers* (New York, 1970).

10 Barry Seldes, *Leonard Bernstein: The Political Life of an American Musician* (Berkeley, CA, 2009), p. 116.

11 Quoted in Burton, *Leonard Bernstein*, p. 395.

12 Leonard Bernstein, *Findings* (New York, 1982), pp. 273–84.

13 Burton, *Leonard Bernstein*, p. 400.

14 Seldes, *Leonard Bernstein*, pp. 120–24.

15 Burton, *Leonard Bernstein*, p. 403.

16 Paul R. Laird, *The Musical Theater of Stephen Schwartz: From 'Godspell' to 'Wicked' and Beyond* (Lanham, MD, 2014), p. 46.

17 Ibid., p. 47.

18 Ibid., p. 48.

19 Ibid., p. 53.

20 Jack Gottlieb, 'A Jewish Mass or a Catholic Mitzvah', *Working with Bernstein: A Memoir* (New York, 2010), pp. 133–7.

21 Peter G. Davis, 'Three Faces of Lenny: The Religious Composer. *Mass* – Few Creative Acts in Recent Times Take So Many Risks and Achieve So Much', *High Fidelity/Musical America*, XXII/2 (1972), p. 274.

22 Harold C. Schonberg, 'Bernstein's New Work Reflects His Background on Broadway', *New York Times*, 9 September 1971, p. 58.

23 Herman Berlinski, 'Bernstein's "Mass"', *Sacred Music*, LXLIX/1 (1972), pp. 3–8.

24 Noel Goemanne, 'Open Forum: The Controversial Bernstein Mass: Another Point of View', *Sacred Music*, C/1 (1973), p. 35.

25 Hugo Cole, 'Bernstein: *Mass*, a Theater Piece for Singers, Players, and Dancers', *Tempo*, CIX (1972), p. 58.

26 Quoted in Burton, *Leonard Bernstein*, p. 406.

27 Sheila Schulz, 'Leonard Bernstein Discusses His Mass with High Fidelity', *High Fidelity/Musical America*, XXII/2 (February 1972), pp. 68–9.

28 Ibid., p. 68.

29 Burton, *Leonard Bernstein*, p. 416.

30 Bernstein mentioned the work as a possibility to a reporter in Palestine in 1947: Arthur D. Holzman, 'Palestine Inspires New Ballet by Young

American Composer', *Boston Daily Globe*, 2 June 1947, p. 10. Robbins also mentioned the play in a letter to Bernstein written 13 October 1958 (Simeone, *The Leonard Bernstein Letters*, p. 408).

31 Meryle Secrest, *Leonard Bernstein: A Life* (New York, 1994), p. 339.

32 Elissa Glyn Harbert provided a fine study of *1600 Pennsylvania Avenue* in her dissertation: 'Remembering the Revolution: Music in Stage and Screen Representations of Early America during the Bicentennial Years', PhD dissertation, Northwestern University (2013).

33 Burton, *Leonard Bernstein*, p. 433.

34 *Bernstein: A White House Cantata* (Deutsche Grammophon 289 463 448–2, 2000), CD.

35 Burton, *Leonard Bernstein*, pp. 433–4.

36 Cothran's hand appears on one page of Bernstein's pre-compositional notes for *Songfest*. Library of Congress, Leonard Bernstein Collection, Box 1073/24.

37 Burton, *Leonard Bernstein*, p. 438.

38 Ibid., pp. 436–41.

39 Personal interview with Leonard Bernstein in Washington, DC, 15 March 1982.

7 'And all the spooks of swift-advancing age':
Music at the Close, 1978–90

1 The quotation in the chapter title is from Humphrey Burton, *Leonard Bernstein* (New York, 1994), p. 497, from a poem that Bernstein wrote to his friend the poet John Malcolm Brinnin.

2 The Bernstein Office supplies a page on their website that shows which years the conductor worked with each orchestra: www. leonardbernstein.com/orch.htm, accessed 18 August 2016.

3 Burton, *Leonard Bernstein*, p. 477.

4 Ibid., pp. 454–5.

5 Ibid., pp. 462–3.

6 Bernstein's manager Harry Kraut attributed this statement to the conductor in: Robert Jacobson, 'State of Ecstasy: Sixty-five this month, Leonard Bernstein Feels He Reaches New Heights with His Multimedia *Tristan und Isolde* Project', *Opera News*, XLVIII/2 (1983), p. 9.

7   Burton, *Leonard Bernstein*, p. 465.

8   Edward Elgar, *Enigma Variations/Pomp and Circumstance/The Crown of India*, BBC Symphony/Leonard Bernstein (Deutsche Grammophon 413 4902, 1984), CD, timing found through Naxos Music Library, accessed 18 August 2016.

9   *Leonard Bernstein Conducts 'West Side Story': The Making of the Recording* (Munich and Hamburg, 1985, 1988), DVD.

10 Joan Peyser, *Bernstein: A Biography* (New York, 1987), p. 464.

11 Burton, *Leonard Bernstein*, p. 509.

12 Meryle Secrest, *Leonard Bernstein: A Life* (New York, 1994), p. 409.

13 Jack Gottlieb, '[Program Note for] Divertimento for Orchestra by Leonard Bernstein' in Leonard Bernstein, *Divertimento for Orchestra* (New York, 1988), p. [v].

14 Leonard Bernstein, 'Program Note', in Leonard Bernstein, *Halil* (New York, 1984), p. [iii].

15 Ibid., p. [iv].

16 Ibid., p. [iii].

17 Bernstein said in our interview on 15 March 1982 – at the time he was working on the opera – that *A Quiet Place* largely concerned typical American speech rhythms.

18 Andrew Porter, 'Musical Events: Harmony and Grace', *New Yorker*, LIX/21 (11 July 1983), p. 88.

19 Andrew Porter, 'Musical Events: Love in a Garden', *New Yorker*, LX/28 (27 August 1984), p. 60.

20 Burton, *Leonard Bernstein*, p. 492.

21 Ibid., p. 453.

22 Ibid., p. 456.

23 Ibid., pp. 456–7.

24 Ibid., pp. 481–3, 489, 502–3, 510–11.

25 Ibid., p. 374.

26 Ibid., pp. 489–90.

27 Ibid., p. 472.

28 See, for example, ibid., pp. 506–7.

29 Ibid., p. 507.

30 The Bernstein Office supplies a list of the musician's honours: www.leonardbernstein.com/honors.htm, accessed 18 August 2016.

31 Burton, *Leonard Bernstein*, p. 490.

32 Herbert Russcol and Margalit Banai, *Philharmonic* (New York, 1971).
33 Nigel Simeone, *The Leonard Bernstein Letters* (New Haven, CT, 2013),
    pp. 564–6.
34 John Rockwell, 'Bernstein Triumphant', *New York Times Magazine*
    (31 August 1986), pp. 14–9, 24–5, and Leon Botstein, 'The Tragedy of
    Leonard Bernstein', *Harper's Magazine*, CCLXVI (May 1983), pp. 38–40,
    57–62.
35 Burton, *Leonard Bernstein*, p. 497.
36 Ibid., p. 511.

8 A Final Evaluation

1 Paul R. Laird and Hsun Lin, *Leonard Bernstein: A Research and
   Information Guide* (New York and London, 2015), pp. 20–21.
2 Ibid., p. 20.

Select Bibliography

Bernstein, Burton, *Family Matters: Sam, Jennie, and the Kids*
(New York, 1982)
—, and Barbara B. Haws, *Leonard Bernstein: American Original,
How a Renaissance Man Transformed Music and the World during
His New York Philharmonic Years, 1943–1976* (New York, 2008)
Burton, Humphrey, *Leonard Bernstein* (New York, 1994)
Burton, William Westwood, *Conversations about Bernstein* (New York, 1995)
Bushard, Anthony J., *Leonard Bernstein's On the Waterfront: A Film Score
Guide*, Scarecrow Film Score Guides, 14 (Lanham, MD, 2013)
Chapin, Schuyler, *Leonard Bernstein: Notes from a Friend* (New York, 1992)
Cott, Jonathan, *Dinner with Lenny: The Last Long Interview with Leonard
Bernstein* (New York, 2013)
Fluegel, Jane, ed., *Bernstein Remembered* (New York, 1991)
Foulkes, Julia L., *A Place for Us: 'West Side Story' and New York*
(Chicago, IL, 2016)
Freedland, Michael, *Leonard Bernstein* (London, 1987)
Garebian, Keith, *The Making of 'West Side Story'* (Toronto, 1995)
Gottlieb, Jack, *Working with Bernstein: A Memoir* (New York, 2010)
Gradenwitz, Peter, *Leonard Bernstein: The Infinite Variety of a Musician*
(Leamington Spa/Hamburg/New York, 1987), first published
in German as *Leonard Bernstein. Unendliche Vielfalt eines Musiker*
(Zurich, 1984)
Gruen, John, *The Private World of Leonard Bernstein* (New York, 1968)
Hunt, John, *American Classics: The Discographies of Leonard Bernstein and
Eugene Ormandy* (London, 2009)
Kopfstein-Penk, Alicia, *Leonard Bernstein and His Young People's Concerts*
(Lanham, MD, 2015)

Laird, Paul, *The Chichester Psalms of Leonard Bernstein*, ed. Michael J. Budds,
    CMS Sourcebooks on American Music, 4 (Hillsdale, NY, 2010)
—, and Hsun Lin, *Leonard Bernstein: A Research and Information Guide*,
    2nd edn (New York, 2015)
Ledbetter, Steven, ed., *Sennets and Tuckets: A Bernstein Celebration*
    (Boston, MA, 1988)
Monush, Barry, *Music on Film: West Side Story* (Milwaukee, WI, 2010)
Myers, Paul, *Leonard Bernstein* (London, 1998)
Oja, Carol J., *Bernstein Meets Broadway: Collaborative Art in a Time of War*
    (New York, 2014)
Peyser, Joan, *Bernstein: A Biography* (New York, 1987, 1998)
Robinson, Paul, *Bernstein* (London, 1982)
Secrest, Meryle, *Leonard Bernstein: A Life* (New York, 1994)
Seiler, Thomas R., *Leonard Bernstein: The Last Ten Years* (Zurich, 1999)
Seldes, Barry, *Leonard Bernstein: The Political Life of an American Musician*
    (Berkeley, CA, 2009)
Shawn, Allen, *Leonard Bernstein: An American Musician*, Jewish Lives
    (New Haven, CT, 2014)
Sherman, Steve J., and Robert Sherman, *Leonard Bernstein at Work:
    His Final Years* (Milwaukee, WI, 2010)
Simeone, Nigel, ed., *The Leonard Bernstein Letters* (New Haven, CT, 2013)
—, *Leonard Bernstein: West Side Story*, Landmarks in Music since 1950
    (London, 2009)
Smith, Helen, *There's a Place for Us: The Musical Theatre Works of Leonard
    Bernstein* (London, 2011)
Wells, Elizabeth A., *West Side Story: Cultural Perspectives on an American
    Musical* (Lanham, MD, 2011)

Websites

The Leonard Bernstein Estate
www.leonardbernstein.com

The Library of Congress's American Memory site, offering an electronic
    window into the Bernstein Collection
http://memory.loc.gov/ammem/lbhtml/lbhome.html

Select Discography and Videography

Few classical musicians have left a larger legacy of audio recordings than Bernstein, and he was one of the first conductors to explore in a major way the possibilities of video recordings. Provided first below are compact disc and DVD versions of Bernstein's works, mostly conducted by the composer. A collection of seven compact discs of Bernstein leading many of his major works is *Bernstein conducts Bernstein* (Deutsche Grammophon 469 829-2, 2002). The second list includes pieces performed without the composer's involvement to provide recorded examples of other major works. The third list includes recordings of Bernstein conducting pieces by other composers generally considered to be among his interpretive specialities. A very large collection of Bernstein's audio recordings, primarily with the New York Philharmonic, including works by many composers, is *Leonard Bernstein: The Symphony Edition* (Sony Classical 88697683652, 2010). A collection of nine videodiscs including Bernstein conducting (sometimes from the piano) works by Beethoven, Ravel, Berlioz, Verdi, Schumann and Tchaikovsky (and his own first two symphonies, *Chichester Psalms* and *Trouble in Tahiti*) is *Leonard Bernstein: The Concert Collection* (Kultur Video D1525, 2005). The fourth list is a selection from Bernstein's catalogue of educational videos.

Bernstein conducting Bernstein

Songfest, *Chichester Psalms*, National Symphony Orchestra of Washington, Wiener Jeunesse-Chor, Israel Philharmonic Orchestra (Deutsche Grammophon D 112052, 1978)

Symphony no. 3 'Kaddish', Dybbuk Suite no. 2, Montserrat Caballé, Michael Wager, Vienna Boys Choir, Israel Philharmonic Orchestra, New York Philharmonic (Deutsche Grammophon 423 582-2, 1978, 1981)

Divertimento, Halil, Three Meditations from 'Mass', Jean-Pierre Rampal, Mstislav Rostropovich, Israel Philharmonic Orchestra (Deutsche Grammophon 4497 955-2, 1982)

Overture to 'Candide', Symphonic Dances from 'West Side Story', Symphonic Suite from 'On the Waterfront', Prelude, Fugue and Riffs, Los Angeles Philharmonic Orchestra, Israel Philharmonic Orchestra, Vienna Philharmonic (Deutsche Grammophon 447 952-2, 1982, 1983, 1992)

A Quiet Place, ORF-Symphonie-Orchester (Deutsche Grammophon 447 962-2, 1987)

Candide, Jerry Hadley, June Anderson, Adolph Green, Christa Ludwig, Nicolai Gedda, Della Jones, Kurt Ollmann, London Symphony Orchestra and Chorus (Deutsche Grammophon 429 734-2, 1991)

'On the Town' Dance Suite, 'Fancy Free' Ballet, 'On the Waterfront' Symphonic Suite, New York Philharmonic (Sony Classical SMK 47530, 1992)

Mass, Alan Titus, The Norman Scribner Choir, The Berkshire Boy Choir, Orchestra conducted by Leonard Bernstein (Sony Classical SM2K 63089, 1997)

The Age of Anxiety (Symphony no. 2), Serenade after Plato's 'Symposium', Lukas Foss, Isaac Stern, Symphony of the Air, New York Philharmonic (Sony Classical SMK 60558, 1998)

Jeremiah (Symphony no. 1), The Age of Anxiety (Symphony no. 2), I Hate Music, La Bonne Cuisine, Jennie Tourel, Philippe Entremont, New York Philharmonic (Sony Classical SMK 60697, 1999)

Trouble in Tahiti, Facsimile, Nancy Williams, Julian Patrick, Antonia Butler, Michael Clarke, Mark Brown, Columbia Wind Ensemble, New York Philharmonic (Sony Classical SMK 60969, 1999)

Others performing Bernstein's works

Complete Works for Solo Piano, El salón México by Aaron Copland transcribed for solo piano by Leonard Bernstein, James Tocco (Pro Arte CDD 109, 1984)

Chichester Psalms, Missa Brevis (also includes William Walton, *Belshazzar's Feast*), Atlanta Symphony Orchestra and Chorus, conducted by Robert Shaw (Telarc CD-80181, 1989)

Arias and Barcarolles, Songs and Duets, Judy Kaye, William Sharp, Michael Barrett, Steven Blier (Koch International Classics 3-7000-2, 1990)

On the Town, Frederica von Stade, Thomas Hampson, Samuel Ramey, Cleo Laine, David Garrison, Kurt Ollmann, Evelyn Lear, Marie McLaughlin, Tyne Daly, London Voices, London Symphony Orchestra, conducted by Michael Tilson Thomas (Deutsche Grammophon 437 516-2, 1993)

Amber Waves: American Clarinet Music (includes Bernstein's Sonata for Clarinet and Piano), Richard Stoltzman, Irma Vallecillo (RCA Victor Red Seal 09026-62685-2, 1996)

West Side Story, Original Broadway Cast (Columbia CK 32603, 1998)

Wonderful Town, Kim Criswell, Audra McDonald, Thomas Hampson, Brent Barrett, Rodney Gilfry, London Voices, Birmingham Contemporary Music Group, conducted by Simon Rattle (EMI 7243 5 56753 2 3, 1999)

A White House Cantata (concert arrangement of *1600 Pennsylvania Avenue*), Thomas Hampson, June Anderson, Barbara Hendricks, Kenneth Tarver, London Voices, London Symphony Orchestra, conducted by Kent Nagano (Deutsche Grammophon 289 463 448-2, 2000)

A Jewish Legacy (includes vocal music and instrumental works: *Israelite Chorus*, 'Invocation and Trance' from *Dybbuk, Psalm 148, Reenah, Three Wedding Dances, Yevarechecha, Halil, Simchu na, Oif mayn khas'ne, Vayomer elohim, Yigdal, Four Sabras, Silhouette (Galilee), Hashkiveinu*, BBC Singers, Rochester Singers, Milken Archive of Jewish Music (Naxos 8.559407, 2003)

Leonard Bernstein's Peter Pan, Linda Eder, Daniel Narducci, Amber Chamber Orchestra, conducted by Alexander Frey (Koch International Classics 7596, 2005)

Bernstein conducting works by other composers

Beethoven, Ludwig van, *Fidelio*, René Kollo, Gundula Janowitz, Hans Helm, Hans Sotin, Manfred Jungwirth, Lucia Popp, Adolf Dallapozza, Karl Terkal, Alfred Sramek, Vienna State Opera Orchestra and Chorus, 1 videodisc (Deutsche Grammophon 00440 073 4159, 2006)

—, *Symphony no. 9, Ode to Freedom: Bernstein in Berlin*, June Anderson, Sarah Walker, Klaus König, Jan-Hendrik Rootering, Bavarian Radio Chorus, members of the Berlin Radio Chorus (GDR) and Dresden Philharmonic Children's Chorus, Bavarian Radio Symphony Orchestra, and members of Dresden Staatskapelle, Orchestra of the Kirov Theatre (Leningrad), London Symphony Orchestra, New York Philharmonic, Orchestre de Paris (Deutsche Grammophon 429 861-2, 1990)

Bernstein in Paris: Berlioz, Requiem, Stuart Burrows, Orchestras and Chorus of Radio France, 1 videodisc (Kultur Video D1354, 2006)

Brahms, Johannes, *Four Symphonies*, Vienna Philharmonic, 2 videodiscs (Deutsche Grammophon 0440 073 4331 9, 2007)

Copland, Aaron, *Appalachian Spring, Rodeo, Billy the Kid, Fanfare for the Common Man*, New York Philharmonic (Sony Classical SMK 63082, 1997)

Gershwin, George, *Rhapsody in Blue, An American in Paris*, Columbia
Symphony Orchestra, New York Philharmonic (CBS Masterworks MYK
42611, 1987)

Haydn, Franz Joseph, *The 'London' Symphonies nos. 100–104*, New York
Philharmonic (Sony Classical SM2K 47557, 1992)

Ives, Charles, *Symphony no. 2, The Gong on the Hook and Ladder or Firemen's
Parade on Main Street, Tone Roads no. 1: 'All Roads Lead to the Centre',
Hallowe'en for String Quartet and Piano, Contemplations no. 2: 'Central Park in
the Dark', A Set of Short Pieces no. 1: Largo Cantabile 'Hymn', Contemplations
no. 1: 'The Unanswered Question'*, New York Philharmonic (Deutsche
Grammophon 429 220, 1990)

Mahler, Gustav, *Symphony no. 1 'Titan', Symphony no. 2 'Resurrection'*, Janet
Baker, Sheila Armstrong, Edinburgh Festival Chorus, London Symphony
Orchestra, New York Philharmonic (Sony Classics SM2K 47573, 1992)

—, *Symphonies no. 7 and no. 8*, Edda Moser, Judith Blegen, Gerti Zeumer,
Ingrid Mayr, Agnes Baltsa, Kenneth Riegel, Hermann Prey, José van Dam,
Vienna State Opera Choir, Vienna Singverein, Vienna Boys Choir, Vienna
Philharmonic, 2 videodiscs (Deutsche Grammophon 0440 073 4091 2,
2005)

Schumann, Robert, *Symphonies no. 1 and no. 2*, New York Philharmonic
(Sony Classical SMK 47611, 1993)

Shostakovich, Dmitri, *Symphony no. 5*, New York Philharmonic (CBS
Records MYK 37218, 1981)

Stravinsky, Igor, *Le Sacre du printemps, Pétrouchka*, Israel Philharmonic
(Deutsche Grammophon, 1983, 1984)

Wagner, Richard, *Tristan und Isolde*, Hildegard Behrens, Peter Hofmann,
Yvonne Minton, Hans Sotin, Bernd Weikl, Bavarian Radio Symphony
Orchestra (Philips 410 447-2, 1984)

Educational videos

The Unanswered Question: Six Talks at Harvard by Leonard Bernstein,
6 videodiscs (Kultur D1570-1 – D1570-6, 1992)

Leonard Bernstein's Young People's Concerts, 9 videodiscs, New York
Philharmonic (Kultur Video D1503, 2004)

Leonard Bernstein Omnibus: The Historic TV Broadcasts on 4 DVDS
(Archive of American Television E1E-DV-6731, 2009)

Acknowledgements

I must first thank Ben Hayes of Reaktion Books, who invited me to write this volume. His encouragement and savvy advice were invaluable throughout the process. After forty years with Leonard Bernstein as a consuming interest, this has been a most gratifying project that has allowed me to broaden my knowledge and understanding of this musician, his varied career and his compositional output. My previous work on Bernstein had been mostly bibliographic or considerations of his music, and I have very much enjoyed the opportunity to contribute a biography on this fascinating figure.

It has been my hope in this volume to provide a brief but distinctive and textured look at Bernstein, covering his character and personal life in addition to the many aspects of his career: conductor, composer, pianist, teacher, author and media personality. Music is a profession where practitioners often cultivate more than one area of activity, but few musicians carved out such a deliberately wide swath as Bernstein. I have benefited from the work of a number of scholars that came before me in this area, especially biographer Humphrey Burton, who in 1994 published a tome that had been commissioned by Bernstein's estate. Burton fashioned a remarkably balanced account that remains the most detailed story of the man's life and work. Other biographies by Meryle Secrest and Allen Shawn also provided me with useful information and perspectives. Nigel Simeone published an outstanding and provocative volume of Bernstein's correspondence in 2013, a collection cited numerous times in this study. Also especially helpful have been many articles in the *New York Times*, a newspaper in Bernstein's adopted hometown that provided coverage and criticism of the musician's compositions and conducting from the time that he first gained fame in 1943.

Many people have assisted me in my long obsession with Bernstein and his music. The topic of my master's thesis at the Ohio State University was the influence of Aaron Copland on Bernstein. I thank my advisor Herbert Livingston for nurturing my love for American music and helping me with my first glimpse of advanced research. While working on that document, Bernstein granted me an interview, and I remain deeply appreciative for the interest that he took in a young graduate student. My dissertation was on an entirely different topic, but I still must thank my doctoral advisor James Pruett at the University of North Carolina at Chapel Hill for sharing his deep commitment to the field and love for the dissemination of knowledge. Since I drifted back towards American music in the late 1990s and started to work on Bernstein and musical theatre, I must thank many for assisting me with time, expertise, delightful collaboration and countless favours: William Everett, Vicki Cooper, Constance Ditzel, bruce d. mcclung, Thomas Riis, Jim Lovensheimer, Michael Budds, John Graziano, Carol Oja, Larry Starr, Stephen Schwartz, Sid Ramin, Jack Gottlieb, Elizabeth Wells, Charles Hiroshi Garrett, Tony Bushard, Erica Argyropoulos, Hsun Lin and many others. I especially thank archivist Mark Eden Horowitz of the Library of Congress Music Division for the many times that he has assisted me with the Bernstein Collection and for the help of Marie Carter of the Bernstein Office with advice and permissions, including permission to quote Leonard Bernstein, Felicia Bernstein and Samuel Bernstein, and arranging permission from Jamie Bernstein. Dave Stein of the Kurt Weill Foundation and Gabryel Smith of the New York Philharmonic Archive were extremely helpful in my search for photographs for this volume. My brother Doug Laird and daughter Caitlin Laird kindly each took a photograph for me. Most of all, however, I must thank my wonderful wife and soulmate, Joy Laird, for her love, warm understanding and constant support in the writing of this book, and indeed in every aspect of my life.

Photo Acknowledgements

The author and publishers wish to express their thanks to the below sources of illustrative material and/or permission to reproduce it.

Photos Bert Bial/New York Philharmonic Archives: pp. 99, 105; Library of Congress, Washington, DC (George Grantham Bain Collection): p. 28; photos William P. Gottlieb (Library of Congress, Washington, DC (Music Division)): p. 50; photos Doug Hamer/Starlight Theatre: pp. 89, 90; photos Paul de Hueck/Bernstein Office: pp. 6, 147; John F. Kennedy Presidential Library and Museum (Presidential Papers, White House Staff Files of Sanford L. Fox, Social Events, 1961–1964): p. 116; photo Caitlin Laird: p. 17; photo Doug Laird: p. 179; photos Paul Laird: pp. 16, 20, 25, 74, 106, 137, 155, 174, 176; photo courtesy Weill-Lenya Research Center (Kurt Weill Foundation for Music, New York): p. 69; photo courtesy Philharmonic Archive, New York: p. 39; photo Al Ravenna (Library of Congress, Washington, DC (*New York World Telegram* and *The Sun* Newspaper Photograph Collection)): p. 79; photo courtesy Steve Wilson/Kansas City Ballet: p. 43.